CW00921125

THE ART OF BUILDING A GROWTH MINDSET

HOW TO BREAK FREE FROM LIMITING THOUGHTS, DISCOVER YOUR HIDDEN SKILLS, AND EMBRACE A POSITIVE MINDSET FOR PROFESSIONAL AND PERSONAL GROWTH

THINKNETIC

CONTENTS

Your 60 Second Review Can Change Everything For Us

Whether you've just picked up this book or have already started reading, we'd love it if you could take just 1 minute to leave a quick review. It's as easy as scanning the QR code or following the short link below.

Your feedback—whether it's about the book's topic or your excitement to dive in—is incredibly important for us. Reviews not only offer us valuable feedback, but they also play a big role in shaping how this book reaches a broader audience.

If you'd like to go the extra mile, consider attaching a photo of the book—whether it's the cover or a glimpse of the content—making your review stand out to other readers.

Your review, even with just a few words and a quick photo, makes a world of difference. Thank you for being a part of this journey!

Christoph M.   *Michael M.*

Founders of Thinknetic

Scan me

Go to: t.ly/taobagmr

Your 60 Second Review Can Change Everything For Us

Whether you've just picked up this audiobook or have already started listening, we'd love it if you could take just 1 minute to leave a quick review. It's as easy as following the short link below.

Your feedback—whether it's about the audiobook's topic or your excitement to dive in—is incredibly important for us. Reviews help spread the word, increase the audiobook's visibility, and allow more listeners to discover the content. Reviews not only offer us valuable feedback, but they also play a big role in shaping how this audiobook reaches a broader audience.

Your review, even with just a few words, makes a world of difference. Thank you for being a part of this journey!

Christoph M.   *Michael M.*

Founders of Thinknetic

Go to: t.ly/thinknetic

Get 100% Discount
On All New Books!

Get ALL our upcoming eBooks for FREE
(Yes, you've read that right)
Total Value: $199.80*

You'll get exclusive access to our books before they hit the online shelves and enjoy them for free.

Additionally, you'll receive the following bonuses:

Bonus Nr. 1

Our Bestseller
Critical Thinking For Complex Issues
Total Value: $9.99

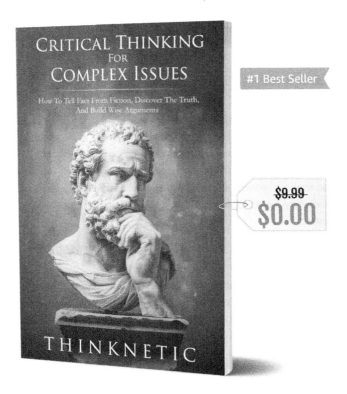

Are you tired of being manipulated by fake news and false arguments?

Arm yourself with the ultimate weapon - critical thinking.

Critical Thinking For Complex Issues is your guide to cutting through the noise and discovering the truth.

Learn how to spot logical fallacies, overcome confirmation bias, and analyze arguments objectively.

"Before this book, I kept falling for online rumors. Ugh! This book explains critical thinking in a way that's super easy to follow. Now I can easily tell what's real and what's fake. Bonus: I learned how to have good conversations, not just pointless arguments. This book is awesome!"

Yvonne - Reviewed in the United States on June 13, 2024

"This short (~300 pages) guide offers a timely challenge to become better thinkers by identifying mental pitfalls that even the best of us can fall into, and how to avoid them. Beginning with an overview of the value of critical thinking in our modern world, the guide then introduces the Socratic approach to asking questions, followed by a discussion on Rhetoric (creating a persuasive argument)."

Thomas Jerome Newton - Reviewed in the United States on July 2, 2024

"This book really helped me to not put trust in everything we might read or hear. Actually it helped me to see how valuable it is to question everything I read and hear. Look at the source, agenda of the information, biased or unbiased etc. Excellent read!"

Jared Szalkiewicz - Reviewed in the United States on June 25, 2024

"This book is very well written which makes it an easy read for those who choose to stray away from the normal path of what I would call herd thinking. Very insightful and provocative. I have already recommended this as a must read to my network of friends and family."

Paul Shelton Sr. - Reviewed in the United States on June 20, 2024

Bonus Nr. 2

Our Bestseller
The Intelligent Reader's Guide To Reading
Total Value: $9.99

Ever feel like you've read a book but can't remember a single thing about it?

You spend hours pouring over pages, only to walk away with a vague sense of what you've consumed.

Imagine reading and actually remembering key arguments. Imagine truly understanding the author's message and discussing it with confidence.

This guide is your secret weapon.

"This is by far the best set of tools and strategies that I've read on improving reading. This is what I wished had been taught in Junior High. I've learned them by trial and error and see how they all fit together."

Michael McFarren - Reviewed in the United States on January 26, 2023

"It's been many years since I've started to regularly read books that I believe would help me grow. A challenge in doing so has been not having a systematic/strategic framework that will help me gain the most out of a book I've read. I'm glad to have found and read this, and after applying some techniques that I have learnt from this book, I already started to experience better results from my reading. I'm sure it will help you the same if you have similar challenge like I did.
Thanks to Thinknetic and its team for their good work!"

Sai Aung Lynn - Reviewed in the United States on April 23, 2023

"This book is very much practical. Straight to the point and concise. Comes with a lot of useful examples to build skills."

Amazon Customer - Reviewed in the United States on December 1, 2023

"I have read books of all types of genres for years. This book has clear and procise ways of reading to help one gain the most benefit out of their reading experience. I recommend all give it a good look there is something to learn for all."

Raymond E. Smith - Reviewed in the United States on March 2, 2023

Bonus Nr. 3 & 4

Thinking Sheets
Break Your Thinking Patterns
&
Flex Your Wisdom Muscle
Total Value Each: $4.99

A glimpse into what you'll discover inside:
- How to expose the sneaky flaws in your thinking and what it takes to fix them (the included solutions are dead-simple)
- Dozens of foolproof strategies to make sound and regret-free decisions leading you to a life of certainty and fulfillment
- How to elevate your rationality to extraordinary levels (this will put you on a level with Bill Gates, Elon Musk and Warren Buffett)
- Hidden gems of wisdom to guide your thoughts and actions (gathered from the smartest minds of all time)

Here's everything you get:

✓ Critical Thinking For Complex Issues eBook **($9.99 Value)**
✓ The Intelligent Reader's Guide To Reading eBook **($9.99 Value)**
✓ Break Your Thinking Patterns Sheet **($4.99 Value)**
✓ Flex Your Wisdom Muscle Sheet **($4.99 Value)**
✓ All our upcoming eBooks **($199.80* Value)**

Total Value: $229.76

Go to the end of the book for the offer!

*If you download 20 of our books for free, this would equal a value of 199.80$

WHAT READERS ARE SAYING ABOUT THINKNETIC

"I have been reading books from Thinknetic for a while now and have been impressed with the CONDENSED AND VALUABLE INFORMATION they contain. Reading these books allows me to LEARN INFORMATION QUICKLY AND EASILY, so I can put the knowledge to practice right away to improve myself and my life. I recommend it for busy people who don't have a LOT of time to read, but want to learn: Thinknetic gives you the opportunity to easily and quickly learn a lot of useful, practical information, which helps you have a better, more productive, successful, and happier life. It takes the information and wisdom of many books and distills and organizes the most useful and helpful information down into a smaller book, so you spend more time applying helpful information, rather than reading volumes of repetition and un-needed filler text.

—Dawn Campo, Degree in Human psychology and Business, Office administrator from Utah

"I came to know about Thinknetic from the Amazon Kindle. There were recommendations for some of the

Thinknetic books. Found every book very interesting. I really loved it. Subscribed for the free material which was delivered right into my inbox. Since then, I have been a fan. I couldn't buy the books... since am in a situation. But as soon as I get a sufficient amount, I plan to purchase some nice titles that piqued my interest. I recommend the books to everybody who wants to live a life free from all sorts of mental blocks that reflect in real life. These books are definitely the lighthouse, especially for those crawling through the darkness of ignorance. I wish Thinknetic all the best."

—Girish Deshpande, India, 44, Master of Veterinary Science, working as an Agriculturist

"I wanted to read some books about thinking and learning which have some depth. I can say "Thinknetic" is one of the most valuable and genuine brands I have ever seen. Their books are top-notch at kindle. I have read their books on learning, thinking, etc. & they are excellent.

—*Sahil Zen, 20 years old from India, BSc student of Physics*

"I associate Thinknetic with critical thinking and knowledge improvement. It is helpful for critical thinkers and all those who are interested in improving their knowledge."

—Elliot Wilson, MBA and Doctor of Business Administration (DBA), Chief Growth Officer

"I have most of the ebooks & audiobooks that Thinknetic has created. I prefer audiobooks as found on Audible. The people comprising Thinknetic do an excellent job of providing quality personal development materials. They offer value for everyone interested in self-improvement."

—Neal Cheney, double major in Computer-Science & Mathematics, retired 25yrs USN (Nuclear Submarines) and retired Computer Programmer

"I've been working my way through the Thinknetic books. It's been a couple months now, and I'm enjoying exploring new ideas and new ways at looking at things. I think these books are helpful for anyone who wants to improve their thinking skills, particularly in business settings. They're also an option for people who are just generally interested in self-improvement."

—Drew Del, Hawaii (USA), 48, Post-grad cert in Education, works as Entrepreneur & Researcher

"Thinknetic embodies an innovative and progressive educational approach, expertly merging deep academic insights with contemporary learning techniques. Their books are not only insightful and captivating but also stand out for their emphasis on practical application, making them a valuable resource for both academic learning and real-world personal development."

—*Bryan Kornele, 55 years old, Software Engineer from the United States*

"I'm a subscriber of Thinknetic for over a year now. I would recommend Thinknetic books to anyone who wants to improve their understanding of cognitive behavioural therapeutic principles."

—Sunil Punjabi, Maharashtra (India), 52, PhD, Psychologist

THE HIGHEST GOOD

"What is the highest of all goods achievable by action?" asks the Greek philosopher Aristotle in the *Nicomachean Ethics*.[1]

The highest good, Aristotle contended, is not a means to an end but an end in itself. It is something inherently good that is pursued not for the sake of attaining something else, the way a job is performed to obtain money, but something pursued *for its intrinsic value*. According to Aristotle, that highest good is human flourishing.

Defining human flourishing, however, is notoriously tricky, as Aristotle himself acknowledged. Perhaps the simplest way to conceive it is functional. Just as the purpose of a knife is to cut and the purpose of a hand is to grab, the purpose of a human is to flourish.

So that we flourish, we are usually told to visualize our most important goals, to imagine a future where everything we have ever dreamed of gains the undertones of reality. These practices require that we generate thoughts, which can be valuable. But I suspect we have singled out our efforts in thought rather than action for the wrong reasons.

We presume that changing our thoughts can be done from the comfort of the sofa, but modifying our actions requires that we endure the thorns that the world may possess. Contrary to the focus on mere thoughts, Aristotle emphasized that human flourishing is not a passive state but a pursuit that requires *action*.

Thus, in the Aristotelian sense, at least three things can be said about human flourishing: It is the purpose of human life, an end in itself, and is achievable through action.

Considering the focus on action, a question may stand out: If it is action that matters, why the hell should you read a book on mindset? There will be more to say, but so far, let's note that nothing happens in isolation. A central premise that underlies the book is the connection between beliefs and actions. As I will argue, beliefs frame the difficulties inherent to the human condition in one of two ways. One leads you away from challenges as it, *a priori*, labels them as threats. The other leads you toward them as it, also *a priori*, frames challenges as opportunities.

Beyond this general philosophical and psychological approach, I should offer some insight into what this book constitutes for the hands that write it. I see no coincidence in my being drawn to the study of the mind. For me, psychological knowledge has not been a mere exercise in abstraction but a way to improve my life when I've needed it most.

In elementary school, when other kids had no trouble learning how to read, I had a reading impairment. In middle school, when other kids could stay in their seats during tests, I had to sit next to my teachers so I could understand exam questions. In high school, when most peers did just fine, I fell behind in several classes and only miraculously graduated without repeating my second to last year.

My interpretation of these scenarios imprinted my character with a sense of doubt over my intellectual capacity. Not completely, because doubts over one's capacity can always emerge, but the scientific study of the mind helped me do away with the spell.

Eventually, I learned to doubt the value of my goals and the ways to achieve them rather than myself. In turn, that led to worthwhile goals to be pursued and efficient means to achieve them rather than to self-doubt.

Armed with more psychological knowledge, I had no trouble graduating college near the top of my class or going through the rounds of competition that any job requires. Fundamentally, I had learned to quit the self-inflicted wounds that limiting thoughts are. In return, I could face difficulties more wholly—with a higher chance of success.

The nature of these stories (and the fact that I've made too many jokes) makes this book something other than a textbook. Instead, it is a practical and empirically supported text with two goals. More narrowly, it aims to teach you everything necessary to develop your intelligence and skills. More broadly, it is an attempt to make human flourishing one bit more accessible through science and philosophy.

Daniel Martín

1

THE RARELY MENTIONED REASON
WHY BELIEF MATTERS

I hated that damn gray line.

I went to high school in Spain back when grades were not computerized, and that was a good thing —at least for the lousy student that I was. My performance in school depended on my grades, but my parents' perception of my performance depended, well, on my words. By communicating only good grades, I could create the illusion of being a good student, which translated into watching NBA games, playing sports, and (rather unsuccessfully) attempting to flirt with older girls after class.

One of my semester's reports, however, marked a short gray line representing a 37/100 in math and a longer one showing a 96/100 in philosophy. Filtering out the math grade would have usually worked, but this time was different.

My teachers became increasingly suspicious, so they asked me to bring back the report signed by my parents. This would effectively end my relaxed student life, but I wasn't going to let the after-class opportunity to talk to Erika and her blonde mane go so easily.

"You know I can just falsify your parents' signature, right?" said my friend Ramiro on a walk back home.

"Use Ramiro, and your parents won't find out you're stupid when it comes to numbers," whispered the devil on my shoulder.

Math, however, was a symptom of an underlying psychological cause. I would be lying if I said my failure was simply an effect of laziness. Instead, a very specific and ingrained belief was at the core of my struggle. I thought that whatever "smart dust" math brains were made of, I had irrevocably missed out on all of it. I also thought I was doing well in philosophy because, surely, I was the next Immanuel Kant.

If you think about it, you can probably identify areas of struggle where you've traditionally believed you lacked the natural talent to do well, much like I did with math. Try to keep those areas in mind as you read through the chapter. It is likely that your approach to them is well covered by what psychologists call a "fixed mindset."

More precisely, a *fixed mindset* is the belief that your intelligence and abilities are set in stone. In this view, you excel at certain tasks because you have a *natural* and *fixed* talent for them. On the other hand, anything you struggle with is seen as something you simply lack the natural ability for.

The Effects Of The Fixed Mindset

Psychologists used to debate the makeup of a human being from two mutually exclusive schools of thought: genetic determinism and the blank slate. The first argued that humans are entirely the consequence of their nature.

"Whatever is in your DNA fully determines who you become," would say genetic determinism.

On the other hand, according to the blank slate, humans are fully the result of environmental influences.[1]

"Given the right environment, anybody can turn into anything," summarizes the blank slate.

Despite the back and forth, it became increasingly clear that both views were inaccurate. You are both nature and nurture. That is, how your traits develop, including your intelligence, is a consequence of how your genes interact with environmental influences.

Having reached some agreement, several developmental psychologists turned to a related question: Do people believe their traits are fully fixed and given by nature (*fixed mindset*), or do they believe their traits can be developed (*growth mindset*)? In landmark studies Chapter 2 will cover, researchers discovered that a fixed mindset leads to devastating psychological outcomes, like giving up on things that deeply matter to you because you fear being exposed as untalented.

We will get to strategies to quit quitting, but so far, it is worth noting that contrary to the fixed mindset, there are ways to develop your skills in whatever area. To do so, *graded exposure* is an optimal strategy. It involves facing whatever you are scared of little by little, and it works through a three-step recipe: identification, reduction, and voluntary action.

First, you need to figure out what you want to improve at. For instance, your capacity to talk to strangers. Then, you have to *reduce* that action to a challenge you are somewhat - but not fully - comfortable facing. We usually miss this step because when we reflect on our areas of struggle, like math was for me, we don't think about the level at which it would be optimal to face that challenge.

Instead, we tend to focus on the level at which we continue to fail. For example, the problems I couldn't solve during tests represent that failure level. Focusing on the failing level makes us feel like we are bad at that particular area when, in actuality, we are just experiencing a *mismatch* between our current skills and what the challenge at hand requires. So, reduce that challenge to a level that more closely matches your skills and, lastly, *voluntarily* face the situation at that level.

If your goal is to talk more fluently with strangers, don't focus on how nervous you get when going into a crowded room to give a public talk. Instead, reduce "talking to strangers" to a manageable unit, like "asking a couple of people on the street what time it is". Then, try to do so voluntarily.

This strategy may seem simple, perhaps almost obvious, but it contains a usually forgotten kernel of truth. The point is to *not* avoid whatever you want to improve at because an optimal degree of challenge is the fuel for growth. But led astray by my fixed mindset, I ran in the opposite direction.

From a fixed mindset, exposure to situations that present a challenge is a threat to avoid because, among other things, these situations could lead to social embarrassment and sharp mental rounds of self-criticism. I thought I had a low and unmalleable amount of math-related intelligence, so I skipped math problems altogether because my mindset—and not the problems—made me feel stupid.

If I had to calculate the check at a restaurant, I'd pull out my phone's calculator. If I had to calculate change at a store, I'd just trust I wasn't getting scammed. Instead, I could have used graded exposure to voluntarily face increasingly difficult math problems, but I never did, so my math skills atrophied, and my gray line got smaller.

Beyond skill atrophy, a fixed mindset also leads to *cheap validation seeking*. If you believe your intelligence is set in stone, you will run away from situations that could expose you as unintelligent. In turn, you will run toward scenarios that *easily* validate you. Although I hid from numbers, I was quick to raise my hand in class whenever easy problems crossed the board. When my teacher asked challenging questions, I moved away from his look.

Having successfully diminished my math skills through avoidance and created a habit of cheap validation seeking, I developed an ingrained sense of intellectual insecurity. One that walked beside me through every high school corridor.

Viewing that short gray line saying "37/100" from this perspective was rather painful. It didn't hurt because it pointed to me as a below-average student in one semester. It hurt because deep within my bones I believed that line could be telling a story about who I fundamentally was: an unintelligent person.

Fixed, But Also False

You likely have a sense that the mind is a powerful entity. Believing in ourselves, we are told, is a good strategy for achievement. And sure thing. If you believe you're the slowest student to ever step into a classroom, that won't help your grades. Your beliefs impact your actions—that's the usual explanation. But that's not the fundamental reason why a fixed mindset makes skill and intellectual development harder.

Your thoughts have what philosophers and psychologists call *intentionality* or *aboutness*.[2] Intellectuals are fancy people (who would otherwise wear elbow pads?), but *intentionality* is a simple concept. All it means is that every belief you generate is *about* something.

For instance, you paint a mental image when the thought sloth crosses your mind. These images may contain either the actual letters in the word sloth or a representation of a slow-moving animal that hangs upside down on trees. Therefore, your mind can be conceived as a theater, and thoughts are the representations that appear on the screen.

Beyond thoughts, you also have *beliefs*, which in ordinary English are interchangeable terms (and we will use them that way to avoid unproductive philosophical headaches). Still, we should note that thoughts and beliefs differ in one regard.

Both thoughts and beliefs are about something (have intentionality)—but only beliefs involve truth. That is, believing something means *taking something to be the case*. For instance, you may believe that sloths, like Sid from the movie *Ice Age*, have big noses. In this manner, thoughts are mere representational objects: words and images that cross your mind. But beliefs are more complex psychological entities as they also involve a "claiming to be true" quality.

It is critical that you understand this difference because even though beliefs claim truth, out there rests a world that can render these beliefs false. To understand why this matters for the development of intelligence, we first need to settle that everything that inhabits the world functions in one or two ways:

(1) As a belief-independent system
or
(2) As a belief-dependent system

Let's look at some examples.

Given that the weather is a belief-independent system, if you are under a cloud that is turning vapor into liquid water, your head will get wet—regardless of what's inside. On the other hand, there are belief-dependent systems, like the stock market, democratic elections, and, most importantly, the development of intelligence.

If enough people believe Elon Musk to be an oracle, stock prices will change whenever he opens his mouth. If enough people believe a candidate will or won't get elected, that will impact the election. And what is more relevant to us: if you believe that your intelligence is set in stone, that will impact your intellectual development, as we will soon cover in more scientific detail.

Trouble, however, doesn't stem from dividing the world into belief-dependent and independent systems. The error comes from treating one kind of system as if it were the other.

Imagine you weren't convinced that the weather is a belief-independent system. Instead, whenever gray clouds hover over your neighborhood, you dismiss umbrellas as nonsense gadgets and go into a deep meditative state to form the unbreakable belief that it won't rain. Doing so would mean treating a belief-independent system as if it could be altered by the contents of your psychology. In turn, you would go through the undesirable outcome of getting your head wet.

The same logic holds for the development of intelligence. At bottom, intelligence can be developed, which we will later argue from brain plasticity. But like I did in math class, many of us treat intelligence as something fixed that you either have or don't have. In doing so, we treat a system that is impacted by our beliefs as if it were something like the weather. However, contradicting this fixed mindset is a rich body of scientific literature pointing to the brain as a *malleable organ* that has the capacity to develop and form new connections.[3]

Therefore, let's keep in mind that beliefs claim to be true, but there is always an underlying reality that can prove your beliefs false. You may take it to be the case that sloths don't hang upside-down trees, but many trees and many sloths, as an underlying reality, would render your belief false.

Figure 1. *The Upside-Down Sloth, renderer of false beliefs. (Photo by Aljoscha Laschgari)*

Similarly, you may believe that intelligence cannot develop, but evidence pointing to the brain as a malleable organ acutely threatens to render this belief false.

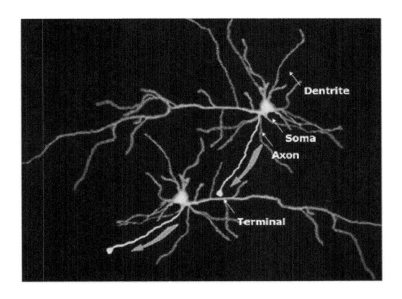

Figure 2. *Two real neurons forming a previously nonexistent connection. The arrows indicate how the electric impulse travels through a neural bridge that did not previously exist.*[4]

<u>The Impact of Falsehood</u>

Beyond claiming to be true, your beliefs are organized in a *belief system* that constitutes a map or model you use to navigate the world. As life progresses, you observe your mind and the world to encounter new information. Whenever you do, you sometimes reject it to maintain your model or map of the world as it was. Some other times, however, you accept new information, which modifies your previous model of the world.

You may want to be a better artist, scientist, entrepreneur, writer, or athlete. Maybe you just need to get by, as I did in math. The fundamental reason why a fixed mindset leads to undesirable outcomes is *not* that your beliefs impact your actions. The fundamental reason why a fixed mindset makes life harder is that, at bottom, a *fixed* mindset is a *false* mindset. It involves treating intelligence as if it operated in one or another way, regardless of what you believe about it. But intelligence is a belief-dependent system. Therefore, treating it as if it were fixed and independent of your beliefs is an inaccuracy in your model of the world.

We have seen how neuroplasticity can give us a neurological basis for the inaccuracy of the fixed mindset, but logic can also be elucidating. To note how the fixed mindset leads to a notorious logical contradiction, let's assume that intelligence is fixed and cannot change. If this were the case, intelligence should *not* atrophy when adopting a fixed mindset, but it does.

As we will cover in Chapter 2, when adopting a fixed mindset we seek easy challenges that stunt our intellectual development rather than more optimal ones that spur our growth. Getting worse or atrophying *is a form of change*, and a fixed mindset denies the very possibility of change, which is contradictory.

This, however, I learned much later. Instead, I used the inaccurate belief that my math intelligence was fixed and equal to zero, so I suffered the consequences. In a self-fulfilling prophecy, beliefs about my inadequacy pushed me away from numbers, atrophied my skill, made me develop fear, and made me frame every math failure as a tell of my math stupidity.

Instead, I could have used more optimal strategies for intellectual development like graded exposure. But because I didn't, I had to eventually make up my mind. I could show my parents a 37/100 in math or ask Ramiro to draw their signature.

I didn't have enough face to falsify my parents' signature, so I put my head down and showed them my grade report. To my surprise, there was no severe reprimand. They were rather constructive and even praised my philosophy grade. My mom also proposed that I thought about what I was doing in philosophy that I wasn't doing in math.

It would be unrealistic to say that this brief but honest conversation turned me into Pythagoras. I never became a world-class mathematician, but honesty had opened a space to explore the false belief that I didn't have what it took to do well in what was not rocket science.

Such a level of honesty steered the ship in the right direction. I realized I viewed myself as capable of understanding complex philosophical ideas. If Kant's sentences, which can be long enough to build a bridge over the sea, were challenging, I saw them as a fun puzzle to be solved. Gradually, I learned to look at math with the same curiosity. I started facing easy problems, then harder ones. That did away with skill atrophy, and eventually, I unlocked the possibility of practice.

It was a slow process because some beliefs can be deeply ingrained, and my high school grades were never stellar. Still, I did better, and as a more aware person, I had no trouble getting As in college calculus and stats.

Ultimately, this is just a brief story, and you have a unique set of challenges that make yours. But in my math struggle there is an overarching insight: Dropping the false belief that your intelligence and skills are set in stone will help you develop.

Action Steps

Think of an area where you have traditionally thought yourself untalented and write it in the margin of this page. Keep it in mind as you read through the book. Do you avoid exposure to this area out of fear, insecurity, or disappointment? If so, you are atrophying your skills because your beliefs are leading to avoidance.

To use graded exposure, identify something you would like to improve, like your ability to talk to strangers. Then, reduce it to a manageable unit, such as asking someone on the street for directions. Come up with challenges of increasing difficulty over time, voluntarily expose yourself to them, and you will eventually make a strength out of a weakness.

Consider how much practice it has taken you to be good at something. Many of the skills you now take for granted resulted from hours of practice and gradual improvement. Anything you consider yourself fixedly "bad" at is likely also an area in which your mindset has prevented sufficient practice.

Chapter Summary

- A fixed mindset is the belief that intelligence cannot be developed.
- A fixed mindset leads to skill atrophy through avoidant behaviors. It also leads to insecurity and cheap validation seeking.
- There are belief-independent systems, like the weather, and belief-dependent systems, like intelligence development.
- A fixed mindset is a false belief because your brain can form new connections and learn.
- False beliefs lead to undesirable outcomes. That is the underlying reason why a fixed mindset causes trouble.
- You have the potential to unlock in all areas, but a fixed mindset makes it more challenging.

2

HOW TO BREED A QUITTER

"**D**ifficulties can lead to failure, and failure can prove me untalented. By quitting, however, I avoid the possibility of failure."

The thought process quoted above is as clear a summary of a fixed mindset as I can offer. Among the many effects of a fixed mindset, quitting is the most detrimental because anything worth accomplishing requires an equally worthy sacrifice.

When thinking that your abilities are set in stone, you start seeing them as jewels to be displayed only before crowds that will applaud them, and that can give birth to self-destructing behaviors. In sports, it manifests as losing games on purpose, also known as *tanking* in the tennis world.

When a tennis player tanks, he or she *intentionally* underperforms. Something that Australian tennis superstar Nick Kyrgios has been guilty of. When facing

Mischa Zverev in the 2016 ATP Shanghai Masters, Nick started to miss on purpose. The official told Nick he couldn't play like that, and fans booed.

He lost 6-3, 6-1, and the Association of Tennis Professionals (ATP) fined him $16,500 for lack of best effort and verbally abusing fans.

"You want to come here and play?!" he shouted back to a fan.

As a professional athlete, Nick has paid a large price to be where he is at. Effort, solitude, doubts, all need to be overcome not so much to get paid and boast about being a professional, but to test your limits as an athlete.

Professionals often seek out those competitive moments when a rival, through their actions, makes it clear that if you want to win, it will have to be over their dead body. These are the moments athletes dream of because that is when you find out what you are made of. But when reaching that very moment against Zverev, Nick let the balls pass.

Tennis purists criticize tanking as an undisciplined act. They claim that the game is to be respected, and fans don't pay to see players miss on purpose. Many have accused Nick of being a narcissist who gives up when challenged, which is a marked fixed mindset trait.

These accusations could make sense if they weren't so obviously half the story. Nick is also responsible for some of the best tennis one can see out there. He has beaten

Novak Djokovic twice in his career, and no fixed mindset quitter can do that.

It can be tempting to point fingers and say someone is either a fixed or a growth mindset person. No such thing exists, however. The line separating the fixed from the growth mindset is not external. Instead, we all approach some situations with a mindset that tilts more toward either the fixed or growth end of a continuum.

Mindset Matters! But What Is A Mindset?

Ask yourself this tricky question: Do your beliefs shape you, or do you shape your beliefs? To answer, we need to understand that a mindset is an *a priori*. Something that, once formed, comes *before* experience. As psychologist Alia Crum puts it, a mindset is a setting of the mind.[1] As such, it determines what you perceive and impacts your behavior, among other influences (like the effects drugs have on you) that we will cover in Chapter 3.

Adding to these definitions, we should note that a mindset is a part of "high-level psychology." Broadly speaking, your mind is divided into lower and higher-order processes. *Low-level processes* overlap with what many psychologists often call the *unconscious*. These processes fall outside of awareness, and you have little to no control over them. For instance, hearing is a low-level process.

You can't be aware of how sound waves make your eardrum vibrate to generate a sound experience later on. Nor do you have control over this process, which is easy to test. If sound waves surround you, you can sit all day and try not to hear something. Nonetheless, if someone drops the key to a xylophone near your eardrum, you will hear something.

Conversely, you have high-level psychological processes that are accessible to awareness and can be controlled—especially if you learn how to. Therefore, a mindset, understood as a set of beliefs, is a *high-level psychological entity*. As such, you can gain *awareness* and *control* over it.

More importantly, you should know that these two sides of your psychology (low and high level) influence one another. For instance, nasty fish smells (low level) influence your moral beliefs (high level), making them more severe.[2] Similarly, your mindset influences your mental health, physical health, and work performance. Considering these effects, let's ask our question again.

Do you shape your beliefs, or do your beliefs shape you?

Just like it was in the case of the nature-nurture debate, the answer is *both*. How relevant it is for your daily life that nasty smells impact your moral judgments is not so evident. But there are other interactions between your high and low-level psychology that do ask for your attention.

Notably, through their top-down influence, your beliefs can impact the development of depression. If you tell people with depression that their condition is fully ingrained in their genes and beyond their control, they get worse. And why wouldn't they? Trying to change something that you think cannot be modified is nonsense. On the contrary, if you tell these patients that depression is, to a degree, a controllable process that they can get out of, their mental health improves.[3]

The same is true of your physical health. In autoimmune conditions like multiple sclerosis, your immune system fails to recognize threats like viruses and bacteria. Instead, it attacks your own body. These conditions *cannot* be cured, meaning that if you have the genes predisposing you to an autoimmune illness, those genes will always be part of your DNA (albeit developments in gene therapy).

Patients initially climb an uphill battle because the first thing they learn is that their condition cannot be cured. However, how their illness develops (their prognosis) depends on their actions to the point where a symptom-free life is possible and, in some cases, probable. When learning so, autoimmune patients realize that they are no longer fighting a nonsense battle, so they engage in activities that increase the odds of a symptom-free life.[4]

Your mindset is powerful enough to turn well-being into illness and vice-versa, but it can also impact other domains like intellectual risk-taking. Because the fixed mindset emphasizes outcomes like being a success or a failure, taking on intellectual challenges is harsher.[5] For example, developing a new scientific theory often requires that you go in front of highly intelligent people to tell them (hopefully through good evidence) that they are wrong.

If you have a fixed mindset, you will frame the creation process as a potential inadequacy-shower. You will be less likely to try to develop new arguments, ideas, or any other creation. In brief, you will be less likely to engage in the vibrant and life-sustaining process that creativity is.

Another effect to keep in mind is that your mindset also impacts how you interpret feedback. If you were to travel them, some avenues would make you a more intelligent and skillful person, and quality feedback makes these avenues more visible to you. But a fixed mindset closes your eyes to feedback, which psychologists have discovered in a set of findings termed the "*Thanks, but no thanks for the feedback*" approach.

We know that fixed mindset people tend to reject feedback, are emotionally hurt by it, and fail to modify their actions. Conversely, when you look at feedback from a growth mindset, it is not emotionally hurtful. Not without first thinking critically about it, but individuals with a growth mindset are also more likely to accept quality feedback and change their behavior.[6]

Once again, it makes sense to connote feedback negatively if you see it from fixed mindset glasses. If you believe your intelligence is set in stone, negative feedback means you are *not* intelligent. Therefore, you protect yourself from the incoming information because your mindset interprets it as a threat to the "smart person" identity you hold so dear.

Such an approach to feedback may sound familiar. It is the one in which you blame teachers for your unsatisfactory grades, the tennis court for your poor performances, or the social system for your financial shortcomings. Although there may be truth to these claims, they are futile if they keep you from considering factors within your control that could improve your situation.

To summarize, we have seen that a mindset is a component of your high-level psychology that can negatively impact your health, creative risk-taking, and feedback framing. And that shouldn't be too surprising. As we saw in Chapter 1, a fixed mindset is a bundle of false beliefs, and the world is harder to navigate when armed with inaccuracy. The effects we have thus far covered are, simply, the outcome of navigating the world with an inaccurate mental model in which your intelligence and skills cannot be modified.

At some level, we know that fixed mindset people, or, better said, *when we fall into the fixed mindset*, we are subject to negative outcomes. But if it is the case that a fixed mindset is so clearly negative, we have an even clearer question to ask.

Why And How Do We Develop A Fixed Mindset?

Nick Kyrgios is the type of athlete everybody praises from a young age. He fits well in the mold of a natural talent as someone who has a high level of God-given ability. He is

6′4″, which gives him an effortless first serve that rivals can barely return, no matter how much Nick went out the previous night. He is also flexible and has good enough mobility to have a complete game.

Like Nick, other professional sports players usually show signs of talent from an early age. The scouts of the sports world are paid thousands of dollars to unveil these hidden gems, and coaches let these players know they have a unique ability.

Through praise, players can be conditioned to see themselves as people who are fundamentally talented. "Being talented", just like "being smart", becomes a core component of their identity. There is nothing wrong with believing yourself talented, but that identity can cause trouble when seen from a fixed mindset.

If you think of talent like I did of intelligence, situations that could expose you as an untalented player are threatening. Nick ended the year ranked 13th globally, while Zverev was ranked 51st. Everybody thought (and thinks) that Nick was a better player, but tennis is a complex sport, and Zverev put up a good fight.

From a fixed mindset, if a supposedly less talented player is beating you, you could be exposed as a failure. So, Nick let the balls pass and missed on purpose because, well, you cannot actually fail if you stop trying.

"Why did I lose? Because I didn't try—it has nothing to do with my talent," is a typical thought process.

"Were I to play at full speed, try my best, wake up early, go to practice, and eat healthy, <u>as my less talented opponent does</u>, I could easily win."

"Were I" is a hypothetical that acts as a shield to protect your talent identity from a reality that could challenge it. These hypotheticals create a set of imaginary scenarios in which things would go right, and these imaginary scenarios provide some comfort because, behind the disguise of hypotheticals, the belief that you are talented is *safe*. That is why a fixed mindset is so common—it protects the idea that we are smart and gifted individuals, and who doesn't like that idea?

I am portraying Nick to be, at times, a fixed-mindset person. However, as I have mentioned, a fully fixed mindset person doesn't exist because it is only *sometimes* that we fall into the fixed mindset. Just like Nick tanked in Shanghai, he has also had stellar performances when challenged.

It is likely that you have traditionally viewed yourself as talented in some areas of your life. Someone who has it, like I did in philosophy. While in some other areas, you have thought of yourself as someone who doesn't have it. Combined, how you view yourself across all facets of your life tilts more toward a fixed or growth mindset.

Therefore, the first part of the question—why do we develop a fixed mindset—has been given an answer: to shield our identity as talented individuals from situations that could threaten it. But the second part of the question remains: How do we develop a fixed mindset?

The main answer, according to developmental psychologists, is the type of praise we receive. Imagine being praised from a young age for how talented an athlete or smart a student you are. Because the brain is a malleable organ, the messages we are exposed to matter. Because the brain is more malleable at a younger age, the influences we are exposed to when we are younger matter more.

In a set of landmark mindset studies, psychologist Carol Dweck showed how the type of praise we are exposed to from a young age can throw us into one or the other mindset. Dweck gave two groups of kids equally difficult IQ questions, and after completing them, she told both groups that they had gotten 80% of the questions right— regardless of their actual score.[7]

"Wow, you did very well on these problems. You got 80% right. That's a really high score."

Afterward, the first group received *talent-related feedback*. This type of feedback is characterized by *labels* like "you are so smart," "talented," or "good." It is also related to the *outcome* you achieved rather than to the process involved in achieving it. For instance, imagine you figured out a smart way to save your company some money. This type of feedback would praise the fact that you saved the company a lot of money. It would also relate such an outcome to some positive label that points out, for example, how smart you are.

On the contrary, *effort-related feedback* ties outcomes to effort and strategies. Coming from an employer, effort-related feedback would point out the *work* you did to save the company money rather than just the outcome of that work.

Praising the first group of students with talent-feedback, Dweck told all of them:

"Y*ou must be smart at these problems*."

The second group received effort-related feedback:

"*You must have worked very hard at these problems*."

When receiving talent rather than effort praise, kids showed detrimental responses. When given the opportunity, talent-praised children chose to do easier problems later on. Thinking their intelligence was tied to their performance, they wanted to perform well, and easier problems meant a better shot at doing so.

These talent-praised kids also reported lower levels of enjoyment while working on the problems and showed a tendency to give up more easily in subsequent problems, which is akin to tennis tanking: You can't be proven unintelligent if you don't try.

When allowed to compare themselves to others, talent-praised kids chose to look at the scores of students who had done *worse*. In this way, they could feel good about being "more talented" than their peers. When asked to communicate their scores to other students, they were more likely to lie and inflate their grades to be seen as more achieving, which feels ironically similar to my high school self.

Lastly, when asked to define intelligence in an open-ended question, talent-praised kids explained it as an internal entity *that couldn't be changed*, while effort-praised kids defined it as something subject to development. I want to highlight that these kids received no information about what constitutes intelligence. They just received a bit of talent or effort praise.

Intelligence-praised kids	Effort-praised kids
Wanted easier problems	Wanted harder problems
Didn't enjoy problem-solving	Enjoyed problem-solving
Were more likely to give up	Were less likely to give up
Compared themselves to lower performers to gain validation	Compared themselves to top performers to find the right answers
Showed a tendency to inflate their scores when communicating them	Communicated scores accurately
Defined intelligence as a fixed trait	Defined intelligence as a malleable trait

Dweck is a careful researcher, so she included several control variables in her studies, which is an important feature to understand. The results in the table above could seem too much if you are skeptically minded, but understanding what a control variable is can help dissipate some doubts.

A control variable is something researchers keep constant in an experiment to make sure it does not impact results. Imagine you had my high school luck with girls and your last date ditched you, but you suspect it was because your armpit smelled a little funny. Lucky you, however, you manage to get another date, and being scientifically minded, you want to test the hypothesis that you were ditched because of your *eau de armpit*.

So, you replicate everything you did on the first date. You go to the same restaurant, wearing the same hairstyle and clothes. Everything is the same, but this time, you make sure your armpit smells like fresh roses. After a similar date, you are having some drinks at the bar, and your date partner utters the magical words.

"Would you like to have the last one... at my place?"

Everything you keep constant—hairstyle, clothes, and restaurant—is what researchers call a *control variable*. These factors cannot explain the different outcomes—being ditched vs. being invited to the apartment—because they were the same on both dates. However, your armpit smell, which has changed from one date to another, can explain the different dating outcomes.

In the same manner, Dweck gave the same IQ questions to every kid, and the kids themselves were of similar ages (10-12 years old), making *question-difficulty* and *age* control variables. The only relevant thing that changed in Dweck's experiments was the praise style, which I cannot emphasize enough because this was a brief experiment.

Little kids were pushed into quitting, lying, and into a fixed mindset *just* with a bit of talent-related feedback. If a brief exercise can have those effects, you can imagine what a lifetime of talent praise can do to you.

Just like your date partner may have ditched you for some other unknown reason, science is not infallible. Maybe there is something researchers are missing when looking at how kids react in different praise scenarios. It is both honest and sound that we mention these potential limitations. However, barring these, our best evidence points to talent praise as a psychologically devastating way to give feedback.

If you are in a position to tell others how they are doing, such as that of a parent, employer, or coach, by all means, tell them. Providing feedback is necessary to achieve anything valuable, but you should tie that feedback to effort and strategies. Don't just praise someone for how smart or talented or innately good they are. Instead, praise them *for the strategy* they used to obtain an outcome and *for the hard work* (if they actually worked hard) that they invested in that strategy.

If you are in a position to receive feedback—by all means —avoid falling in love with talent praise. Talent praise from teachers, coaches, or employers can fade as soon as the positive outcomes do, and that matters because there is variability in the quality of your performance.

You will have some better and some worse tests on some workdays where you will be the epitome of efficiency, and on others, when last night's date is still dancing in your head.

Having better and worse days is inevitable, but talent praise usually ensues *only* from your better days. Someone who falls in love with talent feedback derived only from top-quality performances is meant to be heartbroken when the inevitable fluctuation in performance occurs.

Therefore, it is wise to frame whatever praise you receive in terms of two dimensions. First, as we have said, think about the effort you put into a given task. Second, think about the strategies you used to accomplish a goal. That way, you help yourself develop by controlling how you frame praise. On the other hand, it is wise to give feedback by praising efforts and strategies rather than just talent. That way, you help others flourish through your words.

Self-Determination

Imagine you worked in a company where you were constantly micromanaged. Your boss supervises every click of your mouse and every bathroom visit to the point where your bladder capacity seems like an extension of your work-related skills. Later, when getting home, your over-controlling partner asks, "Where were you, at what time, with whom, and doing what?"

Self-determination theory (SDT) claims that you have three fundamental needs that, when satisfied, foster well-being.[8] These are the need for competence, autonomy, and relatedness. Micromanaging work environments and over-controlling partners feel like a chokehold because autonomy, as SDT claims, is a fundamental human need. The same is true of your need for competence, which asks that you feel capable of doing things successfully and efficiently. And of your need for relatedness, which demands that you have quality interpersonal relationships.

Satisfying these basic human needs is difficult, and a growth mindset will make you face these difficulties with a higher likelihood of success. More importantly, and this is the crucial point, there are factors beyond your control that impact the degree to which you satisfy these needs, but the responsibility to satisfy them, as well as your growth, is yours.

As a more mature athlete, Nick Kyrgios seems to have grasped this same insight, especially when it comes to competence.

"You were at the pub last night, right?" He told a female reporter during Wimbledon 2019.

"You're embarrassing me…"

He still didn't take tennis as seriously as other players. But despite the pubs, Nick stopped tanking. There is no way to know what went through his mind to quit quitting, but a higher degree of awareness tends to reveal a critical insight. As you become more aware, you notice that failing to turn potential into actuality leads to regret, and that realization corrects your behavior.

Adopting a growth mindset and taking responsibility for your actions makes the world feel heavier. There are no more hypotheticals to hide behind. No more imaginary scenarios where you run away from challenges to protect your sweet talent identity.

When dropping the fixed mindset, coming short is always possible; whenever you do, it is your responsibility. That is a heavy burden, but there is a flip side to this coin.

By understanding that you are responsible for whatever you turn into, the world gains a different meaning. Difficulty and opportunity start sounding like synonyms, and you realize that challenges are an inescapable component of life. From this mindset, you face your battles rather than run away. And in doing so, you devise that meeting the unique set of difficulties that make up your life is the prerequisite for growth.

Action Steps

If you were heavily praised for your talents as a kid, take a moment to reflect. Did that lead to avoiding challenges in some areas? If it did, you may have developed a fixed mindset in these areas.

Whenever you face a new challenge, a fixed mindset will make you think that you don't have what it takes. For instance, when trying increasingly difficult tennis drills, a fixed mindset will have you thinking, "I'm bad at tennis." Recall that this is a fixed mindset thought, and whenever you catch that thought, instead of letting it go, reframe it by writing it down as entry 2:

"Today I have thought that (entry 1) <u>*I am bad at tennis*</u> (entry 2). *However, failing is part of learning* (entry 3)."

This strategy will help you reframe the struggle intrinsic to any learning process.

When giving feedback, remember that solely praising talent leads to a fixed mindset. Write your evaluations before communicating them. Then, check whether you are tying outcomes to effort and strategies or are just praising good results through labels like "smart". Evaluating your feedback to avoid only employing talent praise will prevent fixed mindset cultivation. Once again, there is nothing wrong with telling someone they are smart or talented, but our best research suggests that to avoid fixed mindset cultivation, your feedback should mainly highlight *strategies* and *efforts* rather than outcomes and labels.

When receiving feedback, pay attention to the words. If they sound talent-related, don't fall in love with them.

Instead, focus your attention on the effort and strategies that led to a particular outcome.

Chapter Summary

- Your psychology is divided into high and low-level processes.
- Low-level processes *cannot* be controlled and fall outside of awareness. High-level processes can be controlled and fall within awareness.
- Your mindset belongs to your high-level psychology. It impacts your mental health, physical health, creative risk-taking, and the way you frame feedback.
- Praising talent rather than effort generates a fixed mindset. It also leads to lying, quitting, and cheap validation-seeking.
- Self-determination theory identifies competence, autonomy, and relatedness as essential human needs. While meeting these needs can be challenging, it remains your responsibility to do so. Adopting a growth mindset can help you tackle the difficulties involved in fulfilling these very central human needs.

3

EVERYTHING YOU IMPOSE ONTO THE WORLD

I n 2015, my home country was going through a harsh economic recession, having reached a youth unemployment rate of 48%.[1] A situation that led to what was internationally known as the *brain drain*—a mass migration of students and professionals who sought a better future.

My first steps into adulthood made it increasingly clear that my lackluster efforts were going to have a price. I tried to ride the wave and sought to attend college in the United States, but nobody wanted a 37/100 in math.

I could no longer just watch the NBA and chase girls. This time, I had to perform, or else I would face financial shortcomings and the forever-living-with-your-parents that were intrinsic to the younger Spanish generations. Making little money and living with my parents until I turned 30 were not the worst possible conditions; others surely have it much worse, but that's not the future I wanted.

Competitive running was among the many things I didn't take seriously as a teenager, but I thought my legs might be a better way out than my grades. I was right, but I still could not afford the pocket-torturing prices of U.S. universities.

Luckily for me, a school in a small town near the Bronx, NY, offered a partial track and field scholarship. It would put a U.S. education within a manageable price range, but only if I took out a reasonable loan, which I did without second thoughts.

In the military-like discipline of a track team I kept realizing how much time I had wasted. I tried to take the disciplined path, but the truth is, I had never walked it, so it was a foreign land to my feet. Back in high school, I never had any of the many subroutines that go into making you a faster runner. In addition, I had never faced the pressure of hardcore competitions filled with athletes who want to avoid the abrasive burn that tuition poses. I was a newbie, so I easily obsessed over my racing times.

Obsession wasn't terrible; at least now I was focused on a worthwhile end rather than lost. But I had a couple of slow races to start the track and field season in New York. And I didn't know how to manage setbacks.

Slow starts to the season are normal in track and field. The tough pre-season training is too hard on your body and makes it challenging to run fast at the start of the season. But I learned this too late. Instead of interpreting slow times as a natural part of the process, I interpreted them as potential tickets back home.

"If I keep running at this pace," I thought, "I won't get enough scholarship money to finish college."

These were real fears in the sense that the threat they sought to avoid was there. However, through more mature eyes, it seems evident that threats are always present.

Said another way, threats don't justify *maladaptive beliefs*—mental representations that don't correspond to their underlying reality.[2] In my case, the underlying reality was one in which slow racing times were expected at the start of the season. One can start slow and finish the season running fast. Indeed, that's the regular path to fast running. Thinking so would have posed an *adaptive belief*. In essence, one that corresponds to reality, but I wasn't mentally mature enough to grasp these insights in due time.

Instead, I turned caring into obsessing. As I interpreted, I had to fix my running times at all costs, and the solution seemed simple: running more miles. Before practice, after practice, on rest days, on race days. It didn't matter.

I began framing racing times in an all-or-nothing narrative with very little nuance. One in which I believed that running extra miles, even when I needed to recover from races, would lead to more scholarship money. A narrative in which going back to Spain, even when an unemployment statistic is not a sentence to a dire future, was a sure failure.[3]

Interpreting my races in this manner I fell into a psychological trap common to many: that in which you erroneously equate more work to more success without realizing that all quality work is sustained by rest of equal quality.

As it usually occurs when your mind loses control, the body demands that you stop. I pushed the throttle for months, viciously enough to degrade my left kneecap to the point where I could barely walk.

After two semesters of competition, I saw the physical trainer's room more than the track. Physical therapy helped, and my knee got better. But I kept running obsessively because my mental processes had not changed.

Some other teammates also had slow starts to their season but didn't interpret the situation maladaptively. Instead, different individuals interpreted the same information (slow times) differently.

In some sense, we all understand that individuals interpret things differently. However, why we interpret the *same* information differently is not so usually discussed. In this chapter, I will argue that a psychological entity controls how you interpret new information, what meaning you give to past events, and what expectations you generate. This psychological entity is your personal narrative.

All That Comes Before

A personal narrative is an abstract thing. You don't see it, touch it, or hear it. So, let's ask the question that anything so abstract begs. What exactly is a *personal narrative*? It is a set of beliefs constituting a story about where you come from, who you are, and where you are going.

Fundamentally, a personal narrative is a *psychological sensemaking device* that fulfills functions necessary for your survival. As we will cover, your personal narrative directs your attention and tells you what new information means, what past events mean, and what you can expect of the future. Being responsible for these many functions, some psychologists argue that personal narratives are the highest level of human psychology.[4]

Solving what is worth your attention is not an easy problem. The world is filled with stimuli like light and sounds that you cannot perceive. For example, your eyes only detect light of wavelengths between 380 and 700 nanometers. Anything that falls outside the 380-700 range you just can't see, but it's still there.

Evolution has "determined" that only perceiving a subset of all possible stimuli is optimal for survival and reproduction. And that simplifies the problem, but it doesn't solve it.

Among all that is perceivable, you can only pay attention to a limited amount of it. Therefore, your psychology needs to have some mechanism to determine what is worth your attention. As a complex psychological entity, your personal narrative ensures that not everything matters equally. It is a *discriminatory entity*.

Especially today, we live in a tide of stimuli. Companies tell you what to buy whether or not you need their products. Text messages that may or may not be important reach your phone constantly. And romantic partners that may or may not be the love of your life demand (or fail to demand) your attention.

You could pay attention to all sorts of things, and when you don't know what is worth your attention, your brain signals this state as a familiar sensation: *anxiety*.[5]

Anxiety can be conceived as both the anticipation of a negative outcome and a mental signal that tells you there is not enough clarity in your important/unimportant mental filter. That's why planning helps reduce anxiety.[6] It is a way to tell your brain to only pay attention to *goal-relevant information*, which helps impose order on otherwise chaotic information.

Therefore, you can only perceive a subset of all existent stimuli. To solve the attention problem, your personal narrative directs this limited mental resource to only a subset of the tide of stimuli that surrounds you. Once it has done that, it interprets those stimuli—it tells you what they mean.

Unless you are entirely maladjusted, your personal narrative largely depends on the situation that you are in. On my track and field team, we all had similar personal narratives because, at the end of the day, we were all track student-athletes trying to pay for school. As our narratives were similar, we all paid attention to track and field times. Still, given that our narratives were not exactly the same, we interpreted slow times differently.

Whenever I got a slow time, my narrative interpreted them as tickets back home. But other athletes on the team, who came from the United States, didn't have that same extreme narrative. They interpreted the same stimuli (slow times) differently, which is not to say that others had it easier than me.

As enough observation usually unveils, every life has its challenges. Depending on your narrative, new information will gain one or another meaning. Just like I interpreted slow times as a signal to work harder (even when I needed to rest), my teammate Luke, who also started the season slowly, interpreted them as disappointments to his father, who had been a world-class runner.

Beyond directing your attention to a subset of all possible stimuli and interpreting them, your personal narrative also gives *meaning* to past events. I didn't see my lingering poor grades as too big of a deal in high school. But from my new narrative, I interpreted them as obstacles toward a more substantial scholarship in the United States.

I clearly understood that my bad past grades meant an obstacle, but what the past means is not always so obvious. When exploring the past, you may encounter traumatic memories, which pose a particularly harsh psychological challenge, so we tend to set them aside.

Nobody wants to remember the knives that caused a given psychological wound (trauma) in the first place. However, these memories can come back involuntarily and cause distress. That traumatic memories keep coming back is a sign of unresolved trauma, but beneath the painful memories that make it to your awareness, there is something you need to understand.

Recalling these memories is best understood as a component of your psychology knocking on the door of awareness. Something telling you that in those memories lies a piece of knowledge about how the world works. An insight that you have not yet *integrated* with the rest of your personal narrative.

If you explore them in the right dosage you will often see that there is value in these recurring memories. To do so, writing can help. By exploring a traumatic episode through writing you extract the lessons that underlie the pain. You integrate the previously ignored insights into your personal narrative and become a more complete person. And not just psychologically. Voluntarily facing memories of traumatic experiences through writing has biological effects. It strengthens your threat-detecting system—the immune system.[7]

Seeing Your Personal Narrative

Depending on what personal narrative rules over you, you will pay attention to one or another set of stimuli. You will also extract a specific meaning from those stimuli and impose a particular interpretation onto the past. That is why you can expose people to the same information, but they will extract different meanings from it—they have different personal narratives.

Religious texts like the Bible make for a controversial but good example. The text never changes, but our interpretation of it does. Still, we don't need a psychological analysis of the Bible to grasp this insight. Let's look at another example:

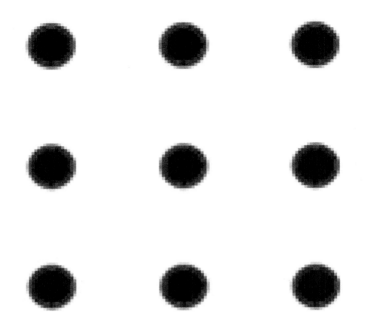

These dots represent an exercise in lateral thinking that only 5% of people get right.[8] The goal is to connect them following these rules:

- You have to use the fewest number of straight lines to connect all the dots.
- You can't lift the pen.
- You can't retrace a line.

For instance, the following solution uses six straight lines:

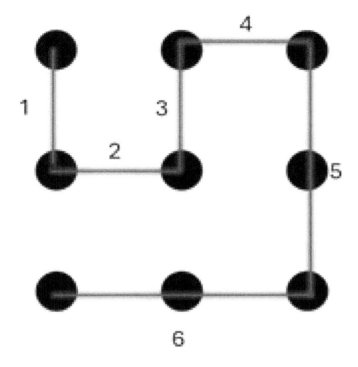

And it is a worse solution than the one below, which uses five straight lines:

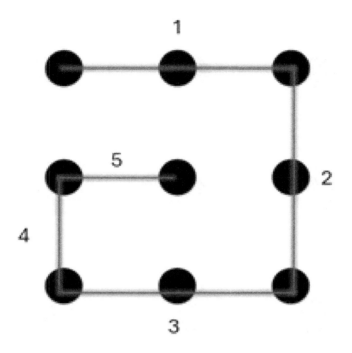

The dots can be connected in a four-line solution, which is hard to come by because a four-line solution contradicts the pre-existing framework you impose on the problem. The framework you a priori impose onto the problem, like most of your psychology, is not directly observable but has real effects.

Note how, when trying to solve the problem, you probably imposed an unconscious square onto the dots. (That's why, at first sight, the dots look like a square.) In addition, you imposed some rules I never mentioned upon yourself.

For example, you tried to start a new line after reaching a corner dot. However, nobody said you had to make a turn after a corner, and there's also no square here - there are only nine disconnected dots.

The solution is hard to find because it involves doing away with a pre-existing framework you impose on the problem. To solve it, you have to *not* see the dots as a square and make beyond-dot turns, like corners A and B below show:

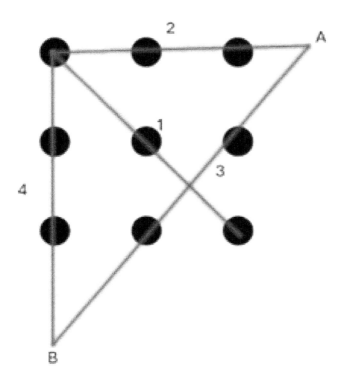

Welcome to the other 95% (?) If you have joined, it most likely means you couldn't do away with your pre-existing framework to solve a problem that required a *different* perspective. As we will cover, the *a priori* square is similar to a personal narrative in that it is simple, pre-existing, and psychological.

The square is pre-existing because *it was not given to you* by the facts (the dots). If you are like the 95% who get this wrong (me included), you had the square in your psychological backpack, imposed it onto the dots, and failed to override its influence to find other solutions. In addition, it is pre-existing, yet simple, because it assigns *no meaning* to the dots; it just mentally unites them.

The mental square you impose onto the dots doesn't tell you that the middle dots are like some others that hurt you in the past and, therefore, should be avoided. Neither does it tell you that corner dots look like handsome devils, the kind you expect to meet at the bar if your gym sessions keep going well.

More complex sensemaking devices, like personal narratives, do extract more complex meanings from new information.

Pre-existing psychological structures, like the mental square and your personal narrative, can lead you astray when they don't adapt well to a situation. Nonetheless, their existence is not in itself detrimental—all the contrary.

As we have seen, your narrative framework serves to structure and simplify the information of an overly complex world that is filled with stimuli. Without a somewhat clear narrative, there's too much to pay attention to, which leads to anxiety and a sense of being lost.

What is detrimental is not the existence of something we can't do away with. Instead, what is damaging is ignorance over the existence of this structure. Contrary to conventional wisdom, ignorance is not bliss. Having no awareness of your personal narrative and how it influences your life makes you blind to what is potentially important. It turns you into an organism blindly moved by the tides of psychological forces within, a mere automaton.

Almost invariably, ignorance of your psychology leads to undesirable outcomes—educationally, financially, socially, and romantically. Outcomes that, ignoring the causes that produced them, you end up attributing to the mystical force of "bad luck". But contrary to ignorance and incorrect attributions is the way of knowledge. And to our purposes, that way runs through a deeper understanding of your psychology and a less clouded awareness of your personal narrative.

Seeing Your Personal Narrative's Framework

You don't come pre-loaded into the world with a particular personal narrative, which is to say that the story you tell yourself about yourself is a learned story. Through interactions with your environment and thought, you develop a set of beliefs that comprise this narrative. Hence, a personal narrative is *learned* rather than innate. What seems to be innate, what you do seem to come preloaded with, is a *narrative framework* that searches for information. Let's clarify.

Just like a square has four sides that are imposed on the nine-dot problem, personal narratives have pre-existing slots that frame new information. We are talking abstractly, but bear with me.

The pre-existing slots from your personal story are the *narrative's framework*. For instance, there is a marked slot we can call *origin*. You fill this slot with information to try to answer an age-old question: Where do you and all this stuff that's around you come from?

You search your environment and mind for information to fill the origin slot, and in doing so, you form a belief about the origin of the world and your personal origin. Different people across history have filled this slot with different information. For instance, some Egyptians filled the origin slot with a story in which the gods accidentally created humans from alternate tears of sorrow and happiness.[9] Vikings filled the origin slot with beliefs about Odin and his brothers using the corpse of the dead giant, Ymir. With his body, they made the Earth, with his blood the sea, and with his skull the skies.[10]

Regardless of the content that fills the origin slot, we all have the same psychological bucket. For that reason, mythological stories from different cultures, irrespective of time and place, differ in their details. Still, because we all have the same origin slot, all mythologies try to explain where things come from through what historians of religion call foundational myths.[9]

In the same manner, your personal narrative has a *destiny slot* that searches for information in an attempt to answer another age-old question: Where are you and all this stuff around you going? In between the origin slot (which tries to answer where you come from), and destiny (which tries to answer where you are going), lies the *identity slot*, trying to answer who you are.

Personal narrative

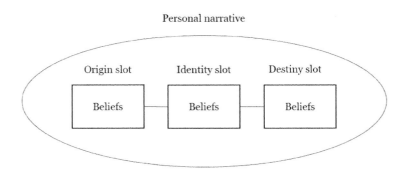

Figure 1. *The narrative framework, common to humans across times and places.*

Once your narrative has been formed and each slot has been filled with beliefs, information inconsistent with each slot's content causes tension. Said another way, information that disagrees with your beliefs is hard to deal with as it requires further processing to be either accommodated within the slots or rejected.

For example, an Egyptian time traveling to Viking Scandinavia would have found it odd that some bearded guys believed the world came from a guy called "giant." And a Viking would have found it strange that Egyptians believed humans came from the happy and sad tears some god cried.

Given that new information has to deal with the beliefs you already have in each of these buckets, the different stages of life can lead to uncertainty and a sense of being lost. In each of life's periods—infancy, adolescence, adulthood, old age—you fill each of the above buckets with specific beliefs. Usually, the older you get, the more observation you engage in, and the more accurate the beliefs in each slot become. However, so that the beliefs within each bucket evolve, you must accommodate new information, which requires an open mind.

You were once an infant that filled the origin bucket with beliefs about a stork bringing babies into the world. Then, an adolescent that, if you were anything like me, filled the destiny slot with expectations about owning a Chevrolet Camaro and meeting Megan Fox.

Similarly, the identity slot was first filled with beliefs about being a student, then a worker, and perhaps later also a parent. More importantly, your growth or fixed mindset are beliefs that fall within the identity slot, as they identify you as either capable of development or incapable. However, throughout each of life's stages, your narrative changes. If it changes well, it adapts more and more to the underlying reality in which you live.

Note how the accommodation or rejection of new information is similar to the nine-dot problem. You already have a square in your mind; thus, seeing an arrow in the dots is hard. In the same manner, you already have an idea about where you came from, who you are, and where you are going. Hence, information inconsistent with this idea is harder to accommodate and, by default, is more likely to be rejected by your psychology.

Lastly, your narrative *generates expectations about the future* because it has a destiny bucket. As we saw in Chapter 1, some systems, like the stock market and intelligence development, are belief-dependent. They work in one way or another depending on your beliefs, and expectations are a type of belief. As such, they influence belief-dependent systems.

Your life, in many facets—financial, intellectual, social—is a belief-dependent system. Therefore, it is worth learning how your expectations impact your future.

The Power Of Expectation

Have you noticed a more prominent age wrinkle in the corner of your eye? If so, how does that make you feel? I hope, well—it is a sign that you are alive.

On average, people who expect aging to be a deterioration process live 7.5 years less than those who expect it to be a wisdom-gaining process.[11] Like Dweck's mindset studies, the experiments that reached this conclusion include control variables (things researchers keep constant), like participant health. Therefore, we can suggest with more certainty that your *expectations* about aging seem to influence how long you live.[12,13]

Beyond aging, your expectations about stress impact how your body reacts to it. In an elucidating experiment, some employees were repeatedly told that stress is debilitating, while others were told that it is enhancing. Over two weeks, those who were told that stress is enhancing reported fewer backaches, less muscle tension, better sleep, and better work performance.[14]

Suppose you expect stress to be physically and mentally enhancing. In that case, you will generate more positive emotion when facing stressors, and your body will produce higher levels of growth hormones—molecules that help you generate new cells and repair damage.[15]

Lastly, as we know from the *placebo effect*, your expectations about a given medicine impact how it affects your body. Morphine is more effective at reducing pain when patients see the injection they are receiving. When the same morphine is administered to these same patients in a hidden manner (through an intravenous tube controlled by a computer), it is less effective at reducing pain. Same substance, different results—all because of your expectations.[16]

The same is true of pharmacological and non-pharmacological treatments for anxiety, hypertension, and Parkinson's. Some of these conditions are severe enough to turn your life upside down, and therapy can be a dollar torture. Yet, your expectations, which fall within your control, have a relevant impact on treatment effectiveness.[16]

Conversely, as we know from the *nocebo effect*, expecting that a treatment won't work makes it less effective.[17] Treatments known to otherwise work for migraines are not effective when patients believe the treatment cannot work.[18] Pharmacological therapies to treat neuropathic pain (pain caused by damaged nerves) fail if you expect them to be ineffective.[19] And drugs to treat fibromyalgia, a chronic illness that generates pain across the entire body, work less if you expect them not to.[20]

The nocebo effect is so powerful that medical researchers have seriously urged for strategies to reduce nocebo responses to otherwise effective treatments.[19] Together, these effects suggest that something as seemingly abstract as your mindset has physical consequences, which can be hard to grasp.

However, that expectations have striking effects on aging, stress, and general health is not magic. Expectations are another high-order psychological entity, and as we saw in Chapter 2, these higher-order entities can influence physical processes through their top-down power. Nonetheless, this I learned much later, and as a college athlete, I paid the price of ignorance.

Other athletes in the team, like the distance runners, had more nuanced and adaptive narratives. They had been running for longer, and part of what makes for a more adaptive narrative is having enough experience so that your beliefs can accommodate an underlying reality more completely. That is, assuming you update your beliefs, the more you interact with the world, the more you discover how it works and generate beliefs that accurately reflect its mechanisms.

In this manner, the distance runners assigned a more functional meaning to their initial slow times. Where I saw my scholarship money tumbling, they saw a natural step in the process. Consequently, no matter how slow their initial races were, they gave their body enough time to recover. In brief, they trained how a mature athlete does: peacefully but relentlessly.

But in obsessively pursuing more scholarship money, I had put that same goal out of reach. After interpreting slow racing times through a non-nuanced narrative and imposing a maladaptive story on the world, I obsessively ran more miles and got injured. Still thinking obsessively, I went through the rehab-to-injury cycle three times. And after just a year and a half of racing, I had successfully ended my young athletic career.

Action Steps

Identify beliefs. Write down origin and identity as column headers, and try to answer the following questions on a personal level: Where do you come from? Who are you? These questions can be answered across various dimensions (e.g., socioeconomically, "I come from Spain, a currently troubled country"). Your narrative is more complex than any single journaling session could allow you to unveil. However, writing it down will help identify what beliefs inform the story that governs your life.

Where do I come from?	Who am I?

Challenge beliefs (part I). Having identified origin and identity beliefs, in a third column, write down what you want out of life financially, romantically, socially, and across any other dimension you deem relevant. You may want financial success but see yourself as coming from an under-favored socioeconomic background, like I did. Maybe you think people from origins like yours don't make it. There can be truth to these beliefs, just like there was truth to Spain's unemployment, but remember, some systems behave in a belief-dependent manner. Just as they impact you, you impact them. Your economic, romantic, and social situations qualify as belief-dependent systems.

Where do I come from?	Who am I?	What do I want?

Challenge beliefs (part II). By contrasting the story you tell yourself about yourself (your narrative) with your explicitly stated goals, you can more clearly see what parts of your narrative are not helping you pursue those goals. In my case, I would have saved myself a lot of unnecessary suffering by factoring in the simple belief that an unemployment statistic doesn't mean I'll have a bad life. This more adaptive belief would have generated hope rather than fear for the future. In the same manner, I would have been better equipped to pursue my goal had I believed that Spain, at the moment, was not the best country to be prosperous—but it was nowhere close to being the worst. Believing so would have generated gratitude, and by having more adaptive beliefs, I would have been better equipped to pursue my goals.

Chapter Summary

- Your personal narrative imposes a structure on the world like the pre-existing psychological square imposes a structure into the nine-dot problem.
- Personal narratives have a set of pre-existing slots (origin, identity, and destiny) that you fill with information.
- Your personal narrative performs several functions: it directs your attention, gives meaning to new information, interprets past events, and generates expectations about the future.

- Your life is a belief-dependent system. Therefore, your expectations about the future impact the quality of your life. For example, aging and stress will be detrimental if you expect them to be.

4

CHOOSE YOUR RESPONSES WISELY

H ave you ever seen a pigeon playing ping-pong? During the 1950s and 60s, psychologists widely focused on observable behaviors rather than internal states like thoughts and beliefs. Given that internal states, like everything you think, believe, desire, or fear, are not directly observable, psychologists claimed they were beyond the scope of scientific study.[1]

This approach, known as *behaviorism*, is further grounded in the idea that environmental influences (stimuli) direct your behavior (responses). Therefore, as behaviorists claimed, stimuli and responses alone should be studied. Behaviorism, however, was more than an academic idea.

Demonstrating how powerful understanding organisms as stimulus-to-response machines could be, American psychologist B. F. Skinner deliberately manipulated the environmental influences that his laboratory animals were exposed to. He tried to modify the behaviors of several animals, most notably pigeons, so they would learn how to play ping-pong.

Doing more than showering you with their digestive byproducts while you wait under a traffic light isn't exactly a pigeon's forte. So teaching them how to hit a ball with their beak to score a point is no easy task. But it can be done.

You first need to place two pigeons in a closed room next to a ping pong table. Then you simply wait—for a long time.

First, the pigeons do what animals do. They inspect the room, fly around, and greet each other. But eventually, they'll get closer to the table. Why the pigeon gets close to the table is irrelevant to the behaviorist. What matters is that it did, and at that very moment, the experimenter rewards the pigeon with a treat.

Treats are a way to tell the animal it's being successful, which initially means just moving toward the ping-pong table rather than away from it. Then, it means touching the ball on the table. Later, it means passing the ball to the pigeon in front, which has been conditioned in the same manner. Gradually, the definition of success evolves from a simple goal, like coming closer to the table, to a more complex one, like passing the ball to the pigeon in front.

If you are patient enough to reward the appropriate behaviors, the pigeons end up playing competitive table tennis. Even wanting to beat each other for getting the ball to go through the opponent—similar to a tennis ace—is also rewarded.

The process by which certain behaviors are rewarded while others are punished or ignored is called *operant conditioning*, and behaviorists employ it to *edit* animal behavior. After enough conditioning, animals that are made to fly will play ping-pong to gain a treat.[2]

Skinner thought the same could and should be done to humans. Whether humans *should* be conditioned according to someone else's will is a question that very well might require a philosophical treaty ("no" is my short answer). However, whether we *can* be conditioned in such a manner according to the principles of behaviorism is no mystery—we can.

Skinner had discovered how to modify behavior and thought that power should be used to improve society. However, such a proposal, or its scientific testing, would raise some ethical eyebrows.

Placing humans in a cage for days and conditioning them to follow a specific behavior would be frowned upon in ethical committees—those that must approve research experiments. But what about books? A book would not raise that many eyebrows.

Under the disguise of fiction, in 1948, Skinner wrote *Walden Two*, a novel where the careful manipulation of environmental influences creates a utopian society.[3]

A little over two decades later, Skinner made the principles to engineer a utopia more explicit in a book called *Beyond Freedom and Dignity (1971).* If you ever plan on ruling the world in a tyrant-like manner or wish to defend yourself against someone who does, *Beyond Freedom and Dignity* is a good place to start.

Skinner argued that humanity has always been filled with problems like hunger, poverty, pollution, climate change, or the overpopulation that some parts of the world go through today. In response to these problems, we have always developed technologies that help us cope.

We try to solve hunger by using more advanced cropping technology, or pollution through less contaminating vehicles. However, as Skinner argued, all human problems ultimately stem from human behavior, and until that is addressed, problems will keep on sprouting.

He thought that if technology could modify human behavior no problems would arise. From this perspective, hunger, poverty, pollution, and overpopulation are the symptoms of an underlying illness: human behavior.

"What we need," writes Skinner when talking about overpopulation, "is a technology of behavior. We could solve our problems quickly enough if we could adjust the growth of the world's population as precisely as we adjust the course of a spaceship."[4]

Being pragmatically minded, Skinner not only told us we needed a technology to control human behavior but also educated the world on how to build it through the principles of behaviorism. Works of fiction like Orwell's *1984* or movies like *Logan's Run*, in which a central authority controls human behavior and even thought, owe much of their conceptualization to Skinner's research. Using the same treat-and-punishment logic that can turn a flying animal into a ping-pong player, your behavior can be modified according to someone else's will.

Manipulating the environmental influences you are exposed to means controlling the news you see, the food you eat, the words you speak, and the work you do. In doing so, your behavior would almost inevitably change.

Controlling the environmental influences you are exposed to would put you at the mercy of the controller's will. And that is a testament to the power of behaviorism.

Writing in 2024, over 50 years after Skinner published *Beyond Freedom and Dignity*, I am forced to ask whether we don't already have the technology of human behavior he foresaw: social media.

The algorithms that choose what to show on your feed use the same ideas that behaviorists developed. These are profitable because they can modify your behavior according to the *a priori* goals of a master—those who happen to rule over the social media platform. These goals usually include increased screen time and monetization, but that's missing the point.

If those goals changed and someone wanted to, for example, manipulate human behavior to win a presidential election, the technological means to achieve them are available.

Arguably, defending yourself from detrimental environmental influences has never been so important. Throughout the book, I have argued for the relevance of taking responsibility for your growth. However, here I come, telling you that your life can be at the mercy of someone else's will—but that's not entirely true.

An environmental influence is more or less impactful depending on how satisfied your needs are. When you are well-nourished in all your needs, you are not so easily manipulatable. For that reason, Skinner deprived his animals so that they behaved the way he wanted. His lab's pigeons had to be starved to 75% of their regular body weight for conditioning to work well.[5] If well-fed, treats to make them play ping-pong wouldn't have been so effective because, in virtue of their nature, pigeons don't care much about ping-pong.

The power of behaviorism ends or is substantially reduced where your well-nourished nature starts. It is known that less socially nourished rats (having a deprived relatedness need) are more susceptible to drug addiction.[6] Or that rats in boring environments, which can be conceived as a deprived competence need, are more easily addicted to cocaine than those that have plenty of things to do.[7] Rodents are also more susceptible to drug intake when they are with other cocaine-using rats than when they are alone, which is the research-intensive way of finding that one is better alone than in bad company.[8]

These animals have a nature, just like you do. Well-nourished in all the needs that constitute your nature, you are not so easily manipulatable. The relevant question, therefore, is this: How can you be well-nourished?

When Things Go Left

Depending on how you respond to a stimulus, you will meet your needs more completely or incompletely. For example, you need social relatedness but may respond to your friends going out without you (stimulus) with bursts of uncontrollable anger (response).

Nobody likes to have a friend who spouts foam at the mouth whenever they are not told about a plan. In response to that uncontrolled anger, your friends will be less likely to invite you next time, which will make you angrier. And that will lead to even less social contact, creating a vicious cycle that deprives you of social relatedness. But there's another way.

You can't always control what you expose yourself to. For that matter, you can't even control how you react to some stimuli, like reflex arcs that are automatic. However, you *can* control your responses to some stimuli, like social rejection. Furthermore, in my estimation, to the degree that they are controllable, you have a duty to control these responses.

Therefore, the influences you are exposed to *only* partially determine your behavior. You can learn, for instance, not to spout uncontrollable anger when left behind.

Behaviorism has its limits because you are not just the consequence of environmental influences—you also have internal needs that can be better (or worse) satisfied. And your responses, as the social exclusion example shows, play a relevant role in nourishing your needs.

Given the importance of your responses, it is worth learning about *coping mechanisms*, which are a set of stable responses to a stressor over time.

When your friends leave you behind, you encounter too much disorder in a room, or you are overwhelmed by work, you respond in a specific way. That specific response, which can involve thoughts, emotions, and behaviors, shapes a coping mechanism you have learned.

For instance, you didn't simply come into the world preloaded with a tendency to engage in emotional suppression when faced with a shouting boss. Instead, while you may have certain genetic predispositions, somewhere between the time you were born and now, you learned to respond in a specific way when faced with specific stressors.

Given that they are learned, the fact that coping mechanisms have an impact on how good a life you live is wonderful news. Although it may take more effort, much of what is learned can be unlearned.

Just as you may have developed the tendency to swallow up your emotions (or burst out uncontrollably) when faced with a stressor, you can learn how to deal with that same stressor in a more adaptive way.

In addition to your capacity to learn and unlearn coping strategies, you should know that not all coping mechanisms are the same. Some are adaptive, while others are maladaptive, which is the overly complex way in which psychologists state that some responses are good for you while others are not. Adaptive coping mechanisms help you thrive and pose actual solutions to problems. Maladaptive coping mechanisms are, at best, postponing your problems and, at worst, magnifying them.

A common maladaptive coping mechanism is *experiential avoidance*, which refers to the tendency to avoid or deny the stressor.[9] It also echoes the difficulty avoidance and skill atrophy pathway that the fixed mindset, scared to confront challenges, paves.

Experiential avoidance is the opposite of the graded exposure strategy we covered in Chapter 1. For instance, imagine you have a romantic partner you no longer want to be with. If you have a tendency to cope through avoidance, you might stop seeing your partner as often, avoid conversations about the relationship, or even ignore their messages. These actions demonstrate behavioral manifestations of avoidance.

Seeing your partner reminds you that the relationship has run its course, and that is a stressor you don't wish to face. Therefore, you also suppress thoughts that remind you of the need to break up and set aside negative emotions derived from the situation.

Avoiding stressors through behaviors or suppressing the thoughts and emotions a stressor elicits can instantly reap results. That's why we do it. If you have no thoughts or emotions arising from your desire to break up, you won't suffer the stress related to the underlying situation. But you are not playing that simple of a game.

If your mind has had to pull the lever of avoidance, this is the part of the game where an obstacle is in the way. The obstacle may be an upcoming breakup conversation you've been postponing, a difficult exam you want to escape, a potential resignation letter, or any of the tribulations intrinsic to being alive.

Looking away is tempting, but that doesn't magically make the barrier disappear. Perhaps it's external in the form of romantic trouble. Perhaps it's internal in the form of traumatic memories you fear accessing. Wherever it's located, it usually blocks a path you must walk to attain something you need.

And I say *need* and not *want* because attaining things we need sometimes requires doing things we don't desire to do. For example, sending that resignation letter and searching for a job that, potentially, will fill the spirit as well as the table.

Avoidance coping can momentarily remove the sensations associated with a stressor, but it doesn't erase it. You stop seeing, thinking, and feeling the stressor, but it is still there—unresolved—waiting for you to face it, causing discomfort from the background it has been relegated to. Since they are maladaptive coping strategies, it should not be surprising that avoidant behaviors, suppressing thoughts, and suppressing emotions lead to higher levels of mental illness.[10]

Paint Reality More Completely

As we will further cover in Chapter 5, the mind has eyes tuned to the short-term, which is a psychological vulnerability.

If you have been thinking about breaking up, your mind tends to underplay how much trouble you are putting yourself in by *not* breaking up. It's easy to see an upcoming breakup as a high-tension point, but it's not so easy to see the accrued effects of an unfulfilled relationship. Similarly, if you have been thinking about quitting your job, your mind underplays how much of an impact staying in a place you don't belong has.

It is wise to defend yourself against this vulnerability through *reverse picturing*, which is a way to paint a more complete image of reality. It is a way to not only divert attention to the short-term benefits of avoidance but also to what would happen if you failed to engage in the actions you know—at some level of your being—are necessary.

Sure thing, nobody wants to be romantically left behind. But does anybody want a partner with an unexpressed desire to break up? Nobody wants to quit their job to try to find something better. But isn't staying where you are equally risky when that's making you miserable? All that follows the "but" above constitutes the reverse and real image your mind tends to ignore.

While reverse picturing defends against short-term psychological vulnerability, I must note that there is no life without stressors. No matter how good we get at defending ourselves from psychological vulnerabilities, stressors are an inescapable component of life. And they're not all to be dealt with in the same manner. Some stressors must be *resolved*, and others must be simply *tolerated*.

You don't always have to prepare for the crusade of a breakup conversation or a resignation letter (solving the stressor). Sometimes, you just need to increase your capacity to tolerate whatever bothers you.

You try to solve a stressor when enough little things that bother you have accumulated, like overcontrolling comments from your partner or cold-blooded emails from co-workers. All these things pile up until they reach a threshold. And once that threshold has been reached, you decide to part ways. However, just like you can decide to do away with the stressor, you can also set your threshold higher, so it is not so easily reachable.

A person with a low stress-tolerance threshold is meant to be drowned by difficulties. Having a low threshold, you may think all that bothers you must be resolved or avoided. Consequently, you fail to realize that if you focused on improving your capacity to tolerate stressors, partners and co-workers wouldn't bother you that much.

Fine-tuning the psychophysiological machine that you are through adaptive coping mechanisms like social support and exercise will show that scenarios that were previously stressful are no longer so. Others may still need to be resolved, but you will be better equipped to choose your responses wisely, which becomes more important the worse your situation gets. To the point where, if you fail to engage in the appropriate responses, some have claimed that you stop being human.

Does It Get Worse Than This?

Even when surrounded by the worst environmental influences—a Nazi concentration camp—psychologist Victor Frankl claimed that we still have the power to choose our responses.

The words "Nazi concentration camp" should be enough to know how harsh an environment is, but Frankl gave us insider information. In his well-known book *Man's Search for Meaning* (1946), he tells of a time when a fellow prisoner was having a nightmare. Being benevolent, Frankl extended his arm to try to wake his fellow and save him from more suffering.

"Suddenly," writes Frankl, "I drew back the hand which was ready to shake him, frightened at the thing I was about to do. At that moment, I became intensely conscious of the fact that no dream, no matter how horrible, could be as bad as the reality of the camp that surrounded us and to which I was about to recall him."[11]

In an environment worse than the worst of nightmares, Frankl claimed that the human spirit could prevail if choosing its responses well. Not without effort, but the power to choose the most appropriate course of action is always available.

Furthermore, Frankl claimed that those who failed to resist the death of the spirit abandoned the human condition to become dispirited beasts—animals only driven by their lower natural need to seek food.

"Under the influence of a world," Frankl keeps writing, "which no longer recognized the value of human life and human dignity […], the personal ego finally suffered a loss of values. […] If the man in the concentration camp did not struggle against this in a last effort to save his self-respect, he lost the feeling of being an individual. […] He thought of himself then as only a part of an enormous mass of people; his existence descended to the level of animal life."[12]

As I have argued, when your needs are well-nourished, you are less susceptible to manipulation. But thinking that we can always have our needs met is wishful thinking. Jobs can be lost, savings can dry up, and economies can collapse. Parents can break up, leave their kids behind, or even die to give their kids a life-start with a lesser likelihood of meeting their needs.

The worst that life has to throw at you can come, and that is a terrifying realization, one that has bristled my mind in fear before. However, at the center of the hurricane is your human spirit, and as Frankl witnessed, it can resist by choosing its responses wisely.

Action Steps

Awareness is the first step toward voluntary change. To change your maladaptive coping mechanisms, you first need to identify them. Intuitively, it is possible that a specific maladaptive coping mechanism came to mind as you read this chapter. If this is the case, it is highly likely that is how you cope with stressors. Write it down as, potentially, your typical coping response.

If you want more rigor in identifying your coping mechanisms, you can use the 26-item Brief-COPE scale.[13]

Actions are risky, but so are inactions. Whenever you have an important decision to make, use reverse picturing. To do so, fill up the following 2x2 matrix.

	"What will happen if I [relevant action]"	"What will happen if I don't [relevant action]"
Short-term		
Long-term		

Through this framework, you will paint a more complete picture of all possible outcomes, thus helping you make better decisions.

Chapter Summary

- Behaviorism was early psychology that focused on observable behaviors, ignoring internal states like thoughts and beliefs.
- B. F. Skinner demonstrated that by rewarding the appropriate behaviors, an organism's actions could be heavily edited.
- B. F. Skinner proposed creating a psychological technology (social media?) to change human behavior and solve humanity's problems.
- An important set of responses are your coping mechanisms, which can be maladaptive (experiential avoidance) or adaptive (reverse picturing, social support, exercise).
- While environmental influences are powerful, you can always choose your responses, as Viktor Frankl showed.

5

WALKING A FINE LINE

> "If you can meet with Triumph and Disaster. And treat those two impostors just the same."[1]

— RUDYARD KIPLING

At the entrance of Apollo's Temple in ancient Greece, the Greeks carved out a set of moral maxims. One of these was "know thyself" (γνῶθι σεαυτόν), by which the Greeks highlighted the importance of what today we would call psychological knowledge. However, the temple's entrance had another equally valuable and usually less mentioned maxim: "nothing in excess" (μηδὲν ἄγαν).

Pain is a necessary experience for growth, and it requires applying the second Greek maxim. From a physiological perspective, your body needs to break down to grow. Whenever you engage in resistance training such as weight lifting, you cause damage to your muscle tissue, which triggers a cascade of physiological responses that tell your body it's time to remodel. That way, the next time the stressor comes, you will be better equipped.

You have to break down muscle to build it. We know that, but the same holds true on a psychological level: You need exposure to stressors to grow.

Anything worthwhile often requires that you meet it at an equally worthwhile level of preparation. And that involves going through the pain of setbacks that a fixed mindset dreads. It requires going through the momentary destruction that difficulties create to rebuild yourself. However, while necessary for growth, pain is a tricky experience.

To feel pain, your nervous system has to engage in an information-transmitting process known as *nociception*. You are filled with sensory receptors called nociceptors that scan your body like a police patrol looking for damage. When detected, these nociceptors in your bones, joints, muscles, skin, and even viscera send a signal through neural pathways to the brain. Later, your brain processes that signal and you feel the subjective experience of pain—which constitutes a protective mechanism.[2]

Evolution has favored this system because it alerts you of actual or potential damage. Broadly speaking, it is a good system to keep you going. You experience pain after situations that, in the environment in which your nervous system evolved, reduced the likelihood that you would survive and reproduce. These situations, however, may not necessarily involve physical damage to your body.

For instance, getting socially rejected feels painful because it is harder to survive when no group wants you. We tend to think that negative feelings should be set aside, but the pain we experience after social rejection is a very adaptive response.

Other things constant, an organism that doesn't feel negative emotion after getting socially rejected is worse equipped to survive than one that does. Negative emotions following rejection thus serve as a signal to adapt your behavior and improve social connections.

Conversely, evolution has placed pleasure as a reward for the activities that, in the context in which our neural architecture developed, meant a higher likelihood of survival and reproduction. For that reason, social acceptance feels pleasant, as being able to cooperate with others means a higher likelihood of survival.

The Moral North Star

How to navigate life is a hard question to answer. You could come to think that seeking pleasure and avoiding pain is a good roadmap to go through the intricacies of life. This roadmap sounds so convincing that famous philosophers like Jeremy Bentham argued that pain and pleasure alone are to guide your actions.

"Nature," writes Bentham, "has placed mankind under the governance of two sovereign masters, pain and pleasure. It is for them alone to point out what we ought to do, as well as to determine what we shall do."[3]

Bentham doesn't just describe how pain and pleasure influence you. He goes a step further and says that these two forces *should* determine how you move through life. He doesn't make a descriptive argument; he makes a normative one.

What you ought to do is one of the central questions of human life. You make financial, social, romantic, and many other decisions. And in all these decisions, the question will be just one: What should you do?

Bentham makes it clear: Maximize pleasure and avoid pain. But it's a bit more complex. As I have mentioned, pain is a tricky phenomenon, for some situations require that we expose ourselves to pain to grow, which is to say that the way of the short-term hedonist is only meant to take you so far.

Bentham recognized this and claimed that the compass that should guide your actions is not short-term pain avoidance or pleasure indulgence. The compass that ought to guide action is whatever maximizes pleasure and minimizes pain for the largest number of people for the longest possible time.

This approach, known as utilitarianism, is not without criticism. For example, it seems impossible to know exactly how an action will ripple in terms of pleasure and pain. How exactly will it impact you and others, and for what duration? This is to say that uncertainty is an inescapable component of life.

Barring limitations, Bentham's utilitarianism is a nuanced strategy and a quality framework for decision-making. Using this framework as a brighter north star for your actions, you will quickly devise that some situations require you to sacrifice pleasure or endure pain in the short term, all so that you and others benefit more and for longer.

I was comfortable in Spain and had well-established social ties. But I had to jump to the Bronx, leave everything behind (including my fixed mindset), and grow to unlock the possibility of a sweeter horizon.

From the moral compass above, we can see how the solution to social rejection doesn't lie in avoiding contact, which eliminates the pain of rejection. The solution to rejection is getting better at that contact through gradual exposure. That is, exposing yourself to pain in the proper dosage. Similarly, the answer to the pain we experience after setbacks is not avoidance but increasing competence.

It is psychologically clear that avoiding stressors altogether is detrimental, as we saw through experiential avoidance in Chapter 4 and skill atrophy in Chapter 1. But counter-arguments deserve a clear voice.

Why not just give yourself to the hedonist way? Why not stay within a fixed mindset, avoid challenges, and live for whatever short-term pleasure you may find? More importantly, if you were to walk the short-term hedonist path, would there be any consequence other than pleasure?

It is tempting to think you are off the hook when avoiding the pains you know should be confronted. But right in those words is the answer: at some level of your mind, you already know what pains should be confronted.

Within you, there is an internal moral entity that judges your behavior. Implicitly, your conscience knows how much growth you could attain if you did the things you should be doing. You can try to fool yourself by avoiding necessary pains and looking just for short-term pleasure. But your conscience is always watching (and speaking).

For that reason, whenever you avoid the pains that are to be faced, your conscience acts like the nociceptors of your nervous system, which detect damage so that the brain generates the pain experience. In the same manner, when you avoid what you know should be confronted, your conscience detects a violation of an internal moral rule that commands you to grow. Then, it sends the subjective experience of regret as a signal that may take some time to make itself noted, but it always does.

Not Yet, And So Far

Contrary to short-term hedonism, the seeds for growth reside in the moments when we face physical and psychological pains in the right dosage. Therefore, evolution has given you a riddle: You have a nervous system that, by default, leads you away from pain and toward pleasure, but growth requires that you expose yourself to some pains in the proper dosage.

One of the central problems of human life is to disentangle in what degree you expose yourself to what pains. This is a question whose full answer may take a lifetime, but in considering its centrality there's already much to be gained. I, however, never reached such a conclusion in my younger college years.

It was the summer of 2018, and after enough obsessive training, I had degraded my kneecap to the point where I had trouble walking without experiencing puncturing pain.

Beyond the physical issue that an injured knee posed, having done my first two college years in a small community college, I would have to find a new school to avoid returning to Spain. I had planned to make my legs a vehicle into a new school, just like I had done in the past. However, just like no school wants the 37/100, no track and field team wants an injured knee, so I gave myself to rehab.

Rehabilitation is sometimes construed as a resting phase in which you give your body time to avoid the stimuli that got you injured in the first place. And that's how I took it.

I stopped running for weeks and started avoiding walking postures that made me experience pain—and it worked. After a couple of weeks, I felt no knee pain, so I tried running. But after the first few steps, there was the puncturing knee pain, saying hello once again.

I couldn't get over it, so I stopped running for a longer period. Worsening the situation, I also experienced negative intrusive thoughts that made the path steeper. Since your body is connected to your mind, physical sensations can trigger specific thoughts without your voluntary control. This is especially the case if you have learned that a phenomenon, like pain, has a given meaning, like "bad."

I believed pain was to be avoided in a rehab process. I also believed pain meant I couldn't run. So, every time I experienced knee pain beyond a certain degree, my psychology produced an intrusive thought that was some version of "You have failed at running."

A runner runs, and I was a runner that didn't run. Therefore, I believed I was a failed runner. Sometimes thought patterns can be that simple. I was also used to running and checking my pace because, at the end of the day, that's what a runner does. Checking my pace, however, was not what I needed then. But the wristwatch felt like an extension of my body that I couldn't get rid of.

Just as physical sensations can trigger intrusive thoughts, so can visual stimuli. In my case, whenever the watch marked a grandpa-like pace, more intrusive thoughts pointing to me as a failure crossed my mind.

"You have failed at running. You will never get back to racing. You are not who you used to be."

These thoughts had made running so stressful that I completely gave it up. Without the natural medicine that movement is, my knee got worse. I never learned in due time the counterintuitive notion that the previous section covered: You have a nervous system that moves away from pain, but some pains are necessary for growth. In this case, for regrowth (rehab).

In the frenzy of ups and downs characteristic of any personal story, I realized how much change must be tolerated to achieve valuable goals. With a bad knee, I had to focus my transfer strategy solely on grades. Unlike in high school, this time I had taken good care of my classes, and a school in upper New York considered me promising enough to pay for my tuition without sports, which to this day still strikes me as a miracle.

By the end of the summer of 2018, I had reached my goal of earning more scholarship money in a strange manner. I had gotten into the United States because of my legs and despite my grades. And I was staying in the country because I had turned into a top student who could not run competitively. Inevitably, I was a different person.

In my new school in upper New York, the identity slot of my personal narrative was no longer filled with running information. Now, I was just a competent student, which is an identity that still feels somewhat alien to me. But that identity (i.e., my beliefs about who I was) eased enough pressure to enable an actual rehab process.

Since I was no longer a runner, I didn't feel the need to run fast or check my pace. So, my psychology generated no failure-related intrusive thoughts whenever I experienced knee pain. In addition, I also dropped the need to check the pace on my watch because I no longer saw myself as a runner. And that allowed for the medicine that running slowly was to my knee.

The same stimuli (running slow) that previously produced racing thoughts about being a failure now produced some more adaptive thoughts. Whenever I experienced knee pain, rather than "You have failed at raining," I thought, "Not yet healed, but keep running."

This is a real story, so no magic healed my knee and turned me into a college track and field champion. The truth is, I never competed again in college, which still hurts to think about. However, I kept running non-competitively, and every time I felt knee pain, I thought, "Not yet, but keep running."

One spring afternoon, after a boring math class of the kind I would've failed in high school, I dared to put my watch back on. To my surprise, I was running close to a competitive pace. In giving myself to rehab with a tender mind, I stumbled upon my goal as a natural consequence of my actions. I had a healthy knee.

The notion of "*not yet*" was crucial throughout this healing process because there is no path without stones. Sooner or later, a failed test will reach your desk, a rejection email will make it to your inbox, and a relationship will break.

Difficulties and suffering are inescapable components of life. Whenever these characters make their periodic appearance, you will be tempted to think you have failed, but note how "*failed*" is a verb that doesn't move.

"*Failed*" doesn't tell you what to do next. It only looks at some past actions and judges them as insufficient. However, by thinking "*not yet*" whenever you experience a setback, you subtly tell yourself that you will accomplish your goal. It simply isn't the time—*yet*.

In addition, if you think "not yet" after setbacks you will prime your attention. By thinking "not yet" whenever you fall short, your attention moves away from the search for information that confirms you are a failure. Instead, it looks for the prerequisites that, if satisfied, will turn "not yet" into "I did it."

Albeit physical constants like Plank's, everything in the universe is subject to change conditions. Matter is subject to certain conditions to remain in one of three general states: gas, liquid, and solid. Whenever certain prerequisites are met, like temperature in the case of water, matter changes from one state to another.

Because the natural world is a Russian doll, the principles that apply at one level of analysis (the physical world) can also apply to others. Just like matter changes its state when certain change conditions are met, so does your life.

By thinking, "I have failed," whenever a setback hits, you keep your attention in one state. And not much happens there—just unmoving matter. However, by telling yourself "not yet," you direct your attention to the change conditions that, if met, will transform your state. But the road doesn't end there.

Just like thinking you have failed is a temptation when setbacks hit, being overconfident is a psychological vulnerability that ensues when you succeed. A psychological vulnerability, as we covered in the previous chapter, is a blind spot by default that makes you vulnerable to misrepresenting reality.

When things don't go your way, you tend to sin from catastrophism, a tendency to think you are a failure and to search for information that confirms so. When things do go your way, you tend to sin from overconfidence, a tendency to think you are "that guy" and to search for information that confirms you will always be.

Much of what makes for strength of character is the capacity to recognize these natural mental tendencies— and to respond to them wisely.

Seeing setbacks as "not yet" counters your psychological tendency to feel like a failure when things go left and the opposite holds for attaining and maintaining anything valuable. Whenever you accomplish something, take some time to take a champagne shower, but don't drown in it. Just like change conditions can be met for desires to turn into actualities, there are change conditions that, if met, will take away what you have accomplished.

Therefore, it is wise to remind yourself of "so far." Whenever you receive good news, remember that, so far, things are going well. However, there is work to do to keep things going well.

"*So far*" subtly tells your mind that some forces must be kept at bay if you want to keep what you have. Once again, it directs your attention to the mechanisms that could turn what you have into what you miss. When you get your next promotion or find your dream partner, the danger is no longer not being enough to achieve your goal —you already have what you wanted.

You have a psychological vulnerability to interpret setbacks as unmovable failure and good news as unmovable success. Hence, thinking of failure and success as a set of change conditions, as a set of prerequisites to be met so that things work out and keep working out will prevent catastrophism and overconfidence. In doing so, you will give appropriate treatment to the two impostors that success and failure can be.

Action Steps

Whenever you receive news about a shortcoming, like a failed test or a rejection email, grab a piece of paper and make three columns.

Goal I was trying to accomplish:	Outcome:	Negative thoughts that have crossed my mind:	Reframing negative thoughts that have crossed my mind:
Getting a new job	Rejection email	"I am not good enough"	"I am not good enough, yet"

In column 1, write down the goal you were trying to accomplish (e.g., "getting a new job"). In column 2, write the news you have just received (e.g., "I have been rejected"). And in column 3, add the thoughts that crossed your mind (e.g., "I am not good enough"). If the thoughts in column 3 are judgmentally negative, like the one in this example, write down the word "yet" next to them. Little by little, this exercise will rebuild your thought patterns to accommodate the reality that setbacks don't mean unmovable failure.

After giving yourself the healthy opportunity to celebrate an achievement, follow the same process above. If column 3 reflects overconfident thoughts like "I am extremely talented," add "so far" to them. Both these exercises, inspired by cognitive behavioral therapy, will prevent catastrophism and overconfidence by directing your attention to the conditions that, if met, will change your situation.

Chapter Summary

- Your nervous system pushes so that you move toward pleasure and away from pain, but growth requires that you give yourself to the right pains in the right amount.
- You tend to think of setbacks as unmovable failures and of achievements as unmovable successes.
- The tendency to see setbacks as unmovable failures gives rise to catastrophism, while the tendency to see achievements as unmovable produces overconfidence.
- Catastrophism is a psychological vulnerability that can be prevented by thinking "not yet" when a setback hits.
- Overconfidence is a psychological vulnerability that can be prevented by thinking "so far" when achievement knocks on the door.
- Using "not yet" and "so far" moves your attention toward change conditions.

6

ON BRAIN PLASTICITY. WHY YOU ARE (PROBABLY) NOT A ZEBRA

 "The mammalian brain is the most complex system in the known universe."[1]

> — DR. GINA TURRIGANO,
> NEUROSCIENTIST

Maybe you have never seen a pigeon playing ping-pong, but what about a zebra giving birth?

After an 11 to 13-month gestational period, the mother zebra water breaks and lies on the grass to breathe heavily. In between inhaling and exhaling, she summons an extra ounce of strength to push life an inch further into the world. After enough panting and pushing from the mother, a baby zebra is born. And as it clearly stands out to any human observer, the foal, unlike humans, can run just a few minutes after birth.

Why can some animals run after birth while others take months, when not years, to just walk? For the foal, running as soon as the umbilical cord ruptures is a survival mechanism. Zebras are non-apex animals, meaning that there are organisms on top of the food chain that have historically fed on baby zebras, like cheetahs.

Faster animals potentially sinking their fangs on your body pose an *evolutionary pressure*. One that selects for baby zebras that can run right out of the womb. Quite the stressful life from its onset, if you ask me.

On the contrary, predators that sit closer to the apex of the food chain, like wolves and tigers, have a more peaceful birth. These are the royal class of mammalian birth-giving, for that matter. Being higher up the food chain, they are under *no* evolutionary pressure to come out of the womb running. Because nobody is waiting to feed on them, their motor cortex, which governs movement, can take longer to develop.

So, while a baby zebra comes into the world *preloaded* with the capacity to run, predators like wolves and tigers take longer to develop such a capacity—they even take some weeks to open their eyes.

Think about that for a second. Some creatures cannot even see when coming into the world while others can run.

"And why the hell do I care about this?" you may fairly ask.

We care about the evolutionary pressures that shaped us into what we are today to keep testing the growth mindset's veracity rather than swallowing it like a slogan. If you were a zebra, the growth mindset would be a death sentence for the simple reason that it would hold less truth. You would be better served by a set of beliefs that reflect reality.

In this hypothetical zebra case, the reality is that you would be coming into the world with a good number of fixed brain components. You would be born with a lot more of what neuroscientists call "hard-wired circuitry" —brain components that *cannot* be changed. But that is not so much how your human brain works.

Human birth is more similar to the birth of apex predators than non-apex creatures like the zebra. Still, it vastly differs from these two.

It has been suggested that the hunter-gatherer Homo Sapiens was an apex predator, and so were its predecessors two million years ago.[2] [3] As we have argued, a spot closer to the top of the food chain helps explain why some creatures are born more underdeveloped. That is part of the reason why human babies are born fully defenseless—they didn't have much of a need to run away from predators.

Saying that human babies take more time to develop is another way of saying that when compared to other animals, our brains are more *plastic*. If a zebra had a brain as plastic as the human brain is, it would need to *learn how* to walk. It would need to develop a skill rather than *coming preloaded* with it. A zebra, however, does not have time for that. But you do.

Let's note, therefore, that when compared to other animals, the human brain is particularly plastic, which hints at the veracity of the growth mindset from a comparative perspective. I know tennis tanking is simpler to grasp than neuroscience, but it is important that we dig into the ground of facts that sustain the growth mindset.

To this ground of facts, we should add the human capacity to walk on two legs. Being a bipedal species means that females have a smaller hip than if they walked on four legs, which translates into a narrower birth canal (walking on two legs = small hips = narrow birth canal). In turn, a narrow birth canal selects for the *early* birth of *smaller* and more *flexible* creatures. That's why human babies are small and, as you have probably noticed, quite flexible.

Neurologically, an early birth means that your brain must undergo considerable development in the world rather than in the womb. In essence, our spot in the food chain and the fact that we are a bipedal species are evolutionary pressures that have shaped the human brain into what it is today: An organ quite capable of change, as the growth mindset tries to reflect.

The Wonders Of The Brain

Brain plasticity refers to your brain's capacity to be molded by external influences. And there is an association between how underdeveloped a species is born (like we are) and how plastic its brain is.[4] That is, generally speaking, the earlier an animal is born, the more plastic its brain is.

Given that your brain is plastic, it can form new connections between neurons, as we saw in Chapter 1, but it can do much more than that.

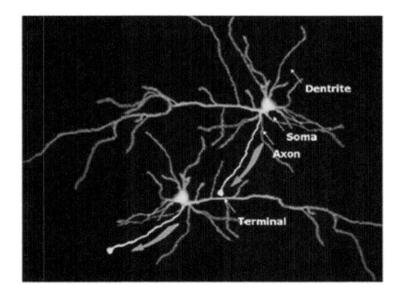

Figure 1. *Two neurons forming a new connection. The arrows indicate the electric impulse traveling from one neuron to another through a previously nonexistent bridge.*[5]

Your brain does not simply form new connections, it is also capable of what neuroscientists call *cortical remapping*. Whenever a set of neurons has suffered damage, the brain "understands" what the responsibility of those neurons was (e.g., speaking) and delegates that responsibility into other neurons.[6] If cortical remapping didn't happen, damage to the neurons responsible for speech would irremediably mean losing the ability to speak, but that is not the case.

In a way, the brain is both the ship and its captain. Whenever something goes wrong in the ship, like water coming in through a hole, the captain restructures the crew (neurons) to avoid sinking. In the same manner, through cortical remapping, multiple sclerosis patients who go through outbreaks of neural damage can still be functional.[7] The task assigned to the damaged neurons is delegated to other functional neurons, and the patient can live an optimal life despite the brain damage.

In addition to remapping, the brain can self-adjust the sensitivity of its neural connections. So that you can do things like moving your legs, an electrical signal must make it from one neuron to another. If the connections between neurons are not *sensitive* enough, the signal can die down. And if it does, you won't be able to perform basic actions like moving your legs when you try to.

Conversely, if the neural connections are *too sensitive*, the electrical impulse can propagate uncontrollably across the neural network, causing an epilepsy-like state. To prevent any of these horrors from happening, the brain must get the sensitivity of every connection exactly right. To do so, it engages in a process known as *homeostatic synaptic scaling*, which is a terribly weird name. All it means is that the brain *self-adjusts* how sensitive the connections between neurons are. When it gets this adjustment right, which is almost always, the electrical signals don't die down or propagate uncontrollably.[1]

Just think about it. You produce a thought that says, "Move right leg," and almost magically, your right leg moves. There is a hidden sea of complexity behind such an apparently simple action. Your thought-to-action command chain works because, among other wonders, your brain has adjusted its connections' sensitivity and gotten them precisely right. We often fail to be grateful enough for how much our organism does to keep us going without asking that we make any conscious effort.

Lastly (and non-exhaustively), your brain can generate new neurons (others also die) in a process known as *neurogenesis*. Beyond brain plasticity, if any finding points to the idea that your brain is not a fixed entity, it would be neurogenesis. Said simply, neuro*genesis* means that you are not born with a fixed number of neurons. You create new ones throughout your life—700 per day in the hippocampus alone.[8] In addition, in the ventricular cavities, more or less in the middle of your brain, you have a good amount of stem cells. These are the clay from which many of your components are made, and they are used to form new neurons that you were *not* born with.

Together, cortical remapping, homeostatic synaptic scaling, and neurogenesis are more than fancy-sounding terms. They imply that your brain is not an entity with fixed physical components like your computer is. Instead, your brain is a very special organ. One that generates new connections between neurons (brain plasticity) and uses backup networks when something goes wrong (cortical remapping). As the most complex system in the known universe, it also adjusts the strength of each connection on the fly so you can go about your day without worrying about it.

It is clear that your brain is not static. Yet, here we sometimes come, with the most complex system in the known universe sitting on our shoulders, ready to doubt our capacity to develop because of our fixed mindset.

The Limits Of A Growth Mindset

Your brain is indeed plastic, but not everything in you is malleable, meaning that the growth mindset has its limits. The brain also has some fixed components, like the neural circuitry responsible for the *palmar grasp reflex* that makes babies automatically grab things. No amount of growth mindset will get you to rewire your brain to stop the palmar grasp reflex because, being a reflex, it is hard-wired and works *independently* of your beliefs.

While not fixed from birth, your brain also has some components that will follow a particular developmental path that is somewhat, and sometimes fully, independent of your beliefs For example, if you don't have the genetic precursors to be 6'8", no amount of mindset or, for that matter, environmental influences, will make you be 6'8" (discounting extremely dangerous surgical procedures, of course).

Environmental influences like proper nutrition will still impact how tall you get, but they do so *in combination* with a set of genes that can get you to 6'8". This is relevant to note because the growth mindset does not mean that you can turn into anything. The following may sound like a stupid example, but it can be elucidating: no matter how much you try, you will not be able to develop into a mature parrot for the simple reason that your genetics constrain you into a human being.

So, let's keep noting that your genes do *not* fully determine what you turn into but they do present a framework. Failing to acknowledge this would be falling into the falsehood of the blank slate, which claims that given the right environmental influences anybody can turn into anything.

Said simply, we should not believe in being limitless creatures. There is a limit to how much your psychology and environment influence what you turn into. But overly focusing on the fact that there are limits to your development would be a mistake. Instead, you should focus on the fact that, while these limitations exist, the upper limit to your growth is *unknown territory.*

To be is to be limited. But to be limited does not mean that the proper strategy to deal with difficulties is falling into a fixed mindset. Imagine waking up, going to work to face a challenging numbers problem, and giving up claiming that this problem is beyond your upper developmental limit. That is the trap.

We often fail to see that momentary difficulties are not the upper limit of our development. Instead, they are just that: momentary. If faced with many of the strategies we have argued, like graded exposure, they will very likely fade.

Grasping such a nuanced view of development is what can make the growth mindset harder to stick. This is also, I believe, the reason why saying that we have limitations rarely makes it to the page in mindset books. Instead, the focus is mostly on how, through the right mindset, you can make it past your limitations. There is truth to that. But there is an upper boundary to what we can turn into. Denying so is part of what can turn otherwise sound self-help books into a kind of motivational pornography that, sometimes willingly, fails to reflect the full picture fearing that it will be pessimistically interpreted.

However, there is nothing wrong with stating the facts. If some of these can seem easily interpretable from a pessimistic perspective, we should change the interpretation, not the facts. This is to say that the growth mindset should occupy a nuanced mid-point between the fallacy that we are entirely determined by our genes (genetic determinism) and the lie that we can turn into whatever we want given the right environment (the blank slate).

Let us be precise and note that there are limits to being human—it seems impossible to *be* something without being limited to that something. Your growth has an upper limit, but the key point is that you have no idea where that upper limit is. For that matter, Aristotle was very keen on pointing out that it is not until one has died that their degree of flourishing can be evaluated.

Therefore, your purpose as a human is to push toward the upper limit of your growth while producing outputs of social value. It could very well be said that discovering where that limit lies is the adventure of a lifetime. Such a journey means pushing to unveil how good of an athlete, musician, scientist, entrepreneur, friend, parent, or child you can be. In that journey, you will often surprise yourself when looking back at how much you have developed. Some other times, you will face difficulties that falsely look like the end of the road. And in this latter case the growth mindset will help.

Those Who Don't Doubt

Figure 2. *1933, a Nazi bonfire of books, which are environmental influences.*[9]

Figure 3. _1933, Nazi soldier reading a soon-to-be-burned book._[10]

As we've explored through various findings, neuroscientists, biologists, and psychologists have confirmed that we have highly adaptable brains. But there is a group of individuals that has never needed so much science to intuitively understand this.

Even if it sounds momentarily strange, the mechanics of authoritarian regimes also reveal that humans possess highly adaptable brains. Authoritarian leaders have traditionally focused on controlling _early_ education and cultural influences as keys to power because they understand that shaping the environment shapes you.

Think about it this way. While your brain does have fixed components, it has so little that is fixed that authoritarian leaders across history have been interested in controlling the messages children are exposed to. Brain plasticity decreases the older you get, but it remains. Thus, authoritarian leaders have also sought to control media, movies, books, and other cultural influences.

To use a paradigmatic example, the Nazis used decrees and laws (ways to modify the environment) to assault the freedom of speech and press that the previous German constitution guaranteed.[11] Fundamentally, they sought to change the environment because, at some level, they understood that environmental influences impact how humans develop.

When I claim that the growth mindset holds truth, I am suggesting that there's good scientific and even historical evidence backing the claim that you can develop. If you were a zebra, I would tell you that the fixed mindset is much more apt. You would have to run away from predators after rupturing the umbilical cord, maybe even before that. You would also be born with a more developed brain to face these challenges. A brain that, on one end, would allow you to run away from predators and to open your eyes early, but on the other, would be less plastic and adaptable.

As you may have noted by (I presume) your lack of stripes and hooves, you are not a zebra. You are a human born with an underdeveloped and, therefore, plastic brain. An organism capable of developing in a seemingly unparalleled way in the natural world. Therefore, let's make room for the notion that we do have limits while not denying the fact that we can develop.

Action Steps

Your brain can form new connections (i.e., it is plastic). That capacity, however, can be heightened. Physical exercise has been shown to improve learning and promote neurogenesis (creation of new neurons).[12] Thus, movement is a way to improve your brain function—especially if it is strength training. We know that strength training, like weight lifting, produces growth hormones that promote better brain function.[13] If you want to improve your brain function, you should consider strength training.

Goal visualization is perhaps the most famous psychological technique for achieving goals, but let's take it a step further. Instead of simply visualizing a particular goal, also visualize the barriers that will be present when you try to accomplish that goal. For instance, getting in shape might be the goal. Visualize that. Being too tired after work, wanting to do other activities, and having no time for exercise. Those are barriers—visualize yourself overcoming these. This technique is a version of *mental contrasting*, which has proven to be effective in changing behavior.[14]

Goal I want to accomplish:	Barriers I will face:
Getting in shape	Being tired after work but still going to the gym

Chapter Summary

- Apex predators are not hunted by other animals. Therefore, they can learn how to walk later, open their eyes later, and go through more extended postnatal developmental periods.
- There's evidence to suggest that humans were apex predators, allowing for the birth of a fairly less capable creature. In addition, walking on two legs makes for a narrow birth canal, which selects for the birth of a more underdeveloped and flexible organism. Thus, when you are born, your brain is more underdeveloped than in other species that need to run out of the womb (zebras) and/or have wider birth canals (gorillas).
- Your brain can form new connections, delegate tasks to other neural networks when it suffers damage, self-adjust the strength of its connections, and create new neurons.
- Beyond scientific evidence, that authoritarian regimes throughout history have targeted

education and cultural influences implies a brain that molds in response to its environment.

- The strength behind the growth mindset is its truthfulness. Unlike zebras, your brain is highly moldable; thus, the fixed mindset holds less truth for you.

7

OVERCOMING STICKY THOUGHTS
AND ACCOMPLISHING BIG GOALS

I hit the right key.

By my junior year in college, I believed myself capable of development, and my schoolwork reflected my more accurate belief. The assignments that, if handed in at all, I would submit late in high school, were on time during college. The NBA games I would devote my time to instead of my homework turned into scientific content from YouTube that I also watched with excitement. And the older girls I would chase, well, that stayed the same.

I feared low grades like I feared slow track and field times, but that fear produced two different outcomes. On the track, it resulted in a degraded kneecap because unless you expect to hit the two laps of an 800m race in zero seconds, you always have seconds to shave off your time. And that, on top of pursuing scholarship money, made for obsessive training.

In the classroom, however, fearing low grades worked well because there's a reachable upper numerical limit to how well you can do in a class (getting 100 points). Thus, I accumulated good grades, and after three years of college, I had an impeccable 4.0 GPA.

"I am turning things around," I thought.

At the start of my fourth year, I was dedicating more time to reading and writing in my spare time than to my actual classes, and that led to my failing to prepare for a stats exam. Echoing my younger self, I got a 47. And, to my surprise, that was all it took for my fixed mindset to return.

It was frustrating. I was among the top students at my university and felt a better ingrained confidence in my intellectual ability. And all it took to erase what I thought was solid was one lousy test in three years.

The thoughts themselves were demoralizing, but what felt more daunting was that I seemed to have no control over these thoughts. As far as I could tell, they snapped automatically without my deliberate control over their generation and cessation, like a TV that turns on and off whenever it wants to.

The father of psychoanalysis, Sigmund Freud, proposed that to rid yourself of psychological trouble, you must look into the past to unroot the cause of the problem.[1] And there can be value in that. As we explored in Chapter 3, voluntarily writing about traumatic events can lead to the closure of the psychological wound through understanding.

Those techniques don't exactly constitute a psychoanalytic approach to mental trouble, but they do, of course, look into the past. Later psychologists, however, argued for a more pragmatic approach.

Chief among this second school of thought was psychiatrist Aaron Beck, who suggested that it's not always necessary to unroot the cause of a psychological issue to do away with it. You don't always have to go through your past to fix a problem. Instead, as Beck proposed, you can take the psychological issue at face value and still fix it.

To do so, he synthesized behavioral therapy, which focused on action-oriented techniques like graded exposure, and cognitive therapy, which focused on thoughts. Beck came to what we today call cognitive behavioral therapy (CBT) through this synthesis, whose principles underpin many of the action steps in each chapter.

Chapter 1 covered how your mind is a theater where mental representations in the form of words or images appear. These components are what Aaron Beck called *cognitions* and are the *cognitive* part or the C in CBT.

More importantly, Beck proposed that these cognitions have an automatic quality.[2] They can appear in your mind without your voluntary control, and, as Beck argued, we tend to be unaware of them.

My fixed mindset and self-defeating thoughts were ingrained enough to have become automatic. I had pumped my chest with the idea that I had finally overcome them. And all it took to deflate my chest was one lousy exam.

While CBT identifies some thoughts as automatic, it proposes that they can be modified in a three-step process. First, you must *identify* the thoughts you want to change.[3] You have to formulate the thoughts you want to modify clearly, which can be done with the self-registering techniques the action steps will cover. Then, you need to *distance yourself* from those thoughts.

We tend to accept the veracity of a thought simply because it pops into our heads. Why, however, should you accept that your fixed mindset thoughts are true? You have had millions of thoughts throughout your life. I see no reason to mark a subset of these thoughts as accurate simply because they pop up in your head. If you think about it, that's rather ridiculous.

Instead, you can test the veracity of any thought by understanding that your thoughts are representations—and not necessarily facts—that appear in the theater of your mind. You wouldn't go to the movies, sit to eat some popcorn, and conclude that every image and word, simply because it's on the screen, is true.

For the same reason, you shouldn't treat a thought as true simply because it pops into your head. What determines the veracity of a thought is not the ease with which it appears in your mind, not even what has caused it, what effects it has on you, or how important you consider it.

What determines the veracity of a thought is the degree to which it reflects an underlying reality. As we covered in Chapter 1, a growth mindset is true because brain plasticity is a scientifically proven and underlying reality.

Generating distance, therefore, refers to the process by which you stop treating your thoughts as conclusions, as ultimate reflections of reality, and start treating them as hypotheses—not true or false until further testing has been performed.

The third and final step is *correcting*. It requires that you take whatever thoughts have popped up (e.g., "*I will never be a good artist*") and test them. The relevant question so far is this: Test them against what?

For our purposes, your fixed mindset thoughts should be tested against the reality that brain plasticity is a scientific fact and that, therefore, you can develop your intellect and skills. Thoughts that do not adapt to this fact misrepresent reality and make it harder to navigate the world.

Through identification, distancing, and correcting, CBT aims to transform you into the scientist of your own mind. Someone who doesn't accept thoughts simply because they appear, but treats them as hypotheses that deserve further testing.

You have had millions of thoughts throughout your life, and you do yourself a disservice by granting a subset of these thoughts—your self-defeating thoughts—a special status. One in which you instantly accept their accuracy.

Thus, treat self-defeating thoughts as a fleeting voice rather than a ruling master. For that matter, even growth mindset-oriented thoughts should be treated as a voice that deserves further investigation. The contrary would be dogmatic.

What makes for a ruling master is not one, two, or twenty disconnected thoughts that either sound positive or negative. What makes for a ruling master, and a good one, is a nuanced belief system that you have tested for truthfulness against reality. The belief system resulting from these tests will be a good map to navigate the world.

Behavior, Not Just Mindset

You don't achieve the growth you seek because you change your beliefs—that's an incomplete explanation. You achieve the growth you seek because, by changing your beliefs, you change your behavior. As I noted in the foreword, "The Highest Good," action, and not just thoughts, leads to flourishing.

I didn't improve my math scores because I had adopted the reality-concordant belief that I could develop my math skills. I adopted such a mindset, and that changed my behavior from avoiding to embracing setbacks. Over time, that turned 37s into As.

That beliefs don't directly impact outcomes means that what we have referred to, for simplicity, as belief-dependent and independent systems are *behavior-dependent* and independent systems. If your thoughts about the stock market didn't transfer into behaviors (selling or buying), the stock price wouldn't change. The same holds for presidential elections, the development of intelligence, or any other belief-dependent system.

"This is," says neuroscientist Andrew Huberman when referring to the importance of behavior, "the Holy Grail of neuroscience."[4]

Consider your nervous system to grasp the power of behavior more than intuitively. It underpins every one of your thoughts, behaviors, and emotions, but it will be nothing but dust after enough time has passed. It's a pile of organic wires distributed across your body to transmit information. A bunch of wires that will decompose without leaving a trace of who you are. Therefore, unless you engage in behaviors that leave a record, like writing, painting, or leaving videos stored in a physical system, there will be no way to tell who you are, and that's a pity.

You see the world in a unique way, have faced your unique version of the tribulations that life presents, and have likely found answers that others can benefit from. While going through the economic challenge of finding and staying at a college in the United States, I often remembered my great-grandfather, who left a book about his difficult upbringing in the 1920s developing Spain.

As he narrates, his village had 19 houses, a church, and no electricity. Instead, his mom had to make wax candlelights. Cattle were crucial for the village's survival, so he would often sleep in the stable near the pregnant cows, just in case he had to aid them during birth.[5]

He's my family, but I never met him. He never published his book, but he engaged in the behavior of writing, and that enabled a window into his mind that I could visit when needing help. As he wrote, his village had nothing interesting, but if one focused long enough, one would always find good things. It's to all these good things that he dedicates his book. Chief among them, and what I took to heart, was that despite everybody being poor—by 1920s standards—nobody complained about it.

Leaving something of value behind is a worthwhile goal that requires action and not just mindset. Still, I don't intend to argue that leaving an accessible legacy is the sole purpose of human life. There is much value in behaviors that will not leave a record. For instance, pushing aside the storm of daily tasks to call to those who care about us.

More explicitly stated, you change the world and yourself directly through your actions and only indirectly through your beliefs. Mindset matters, but behavior, whether to leave a record or engage in delible yet valuable actions, is king.

I note the importance of behavior because it is possible that your beliefs about your intelligence and skills—even if you want to change them—won't be easily shaken.

CBT can help, and brain plasticity suggests that you can change your mind, but psychologists have also documented how hard it can be to change ingrained beliefs.[6]

When it comes to a specific domain, like math was for me, you may have undermined yourself in thousands of thoughts.

"I'm not as naturally talented as others," "I'm mediocre."

These thoughts may have run through your mind thousands of times—and that matters. In a significant way, how you see yourself and who you ultimately become are a consequence of your daily thoughts. These are water running through a riverbed. How you see yourself and who you become is the erosion pattern at the bottom of the river.

Any psychology we discuss can be a turning point. However, compared to the flood that a lifetime of self-defeating thoughts can be, eight chapters worth of psychology might be but raindrops in your river. The action steps under each chapter are there for that reason: to avoid that any usefulness you may find in these chapters turns into mere memories. But we can take it a step further.

Accomplishing Difficult Goals

Let's talk about success. Why do equally smart people achieve different levels of success? Maybe they're equally smart but unequally attractive. Perhaps some people are healthier and more intelligent in social situations than others. These traits impact success, but grit is more important than any of them to achieve your goals.

Grit is the sustained application of effort toward a long-term goal. It is one of the best predictors of achievement, which is remarkable. How gritty you are—how sustained is your effort—is more important to achievement than, for instance, your IQ.[7]

In a series of studies, psychologist Angela Duckworth looked at national spelling champions, cadets at West Point, salespeople at private companies, and teachers.[3][8] Across all disciplines, grit was a better predictor of success than IQ, social intelligence, and physical health.

But still. We all know there are things beyond being good at navigating the social world, staying healthy, and IQ that impact achievement. For instance, you may have noticed how the sexy co-worker gets more easily promoted. It is well-documented that attractive people receive a market premium in the form of economic rewards, and that uglier people even have higher chances of ending up in jail.[9] Truly, this can be very demoralizing.

You are diligent in your daily tasks, and here comes your co-worker with their high cheekbones, ready to get promoted. Duckworth's data, however, paints a more promising story, as grit is also a better predictor of success than good looks.

Additionally, how gritty you are is tied to interest and meaning. Interest can be conceived as a function of attention. An activity, like studying high school math, can be something your attention naturally gravitates toward (not my case). Conversely, it can also be something you have to force yourself to focus on.

Accomplishing challenging goals requires a lot of effort, and being interested in what you do makes those efforts feel lighter. However, aligning your goals with what you find intrinsically interesting doesn't imply perpetual happiness.

A significant error of our time is confusing happiness with meaning.[10] Happiness, which we pursue like the donkey chases the carrot, is a short-term kick of positive emotion. A fleeting experience that runs through your fingers as soon as you try to grab it. Pursuing happiness leads to desolation when you find out that, inevitably, there are moments of negative emotion associated with any pursuit.

Meaning, on the other hand, offers more permanence and is a more sensible pursuit. Interest makes your efforts feel lighter, but meaning justifies whatever weight remains to be carried.

After my 47 in Stats, I saw the uglier face of the thoughts that so frequently had visited me in high school. I didn't know about CBT then, so I failed to discern that my returning fixed mindset thoughts were transient visitors to my mind rather than immutable truths. Still, I remembered why I was so far away from home. I remembered my great-grandfather, his sleepovers at the stable, and his mom's candlelights. I remembered my parents, cheering for me three thousand and five hundred miles away.

I recall thinking what every son thinks every now and then. One day, hopefully sooner rather than later, my parents will retire. On another day, their physical health will decay. And from that day on, they will need their son to care for them. When that day comes, whether or not I'll be ready depends on what I do today. And that's exactly the conclusion I reached back then.

As I noticed, success is not so much a function of material achievement, but of how much we can do for others. And those two things are not always the same. As soon as I aligned the caring-for-my-family macro goal to the doing-well-in-stats micro goal, the challenge became surmountable.

If I wanted to keep my perfect grade point average, I couldn't miss a single exam point in three months. And because we can carry the weight when finding the right reasons, I didn't miss a single point in three months.

Action Steps

There are limitations to questionnaires as methods to assess psychological traits.[11] However, these questionnaires are carefully developed and well-tested to ensure they measure what they have to measure. You can take the 10-question Grit Scale to know how gritty you are.

(I) *Identification.* As I mentioned, identification is the first step to changing fixed mindset thoughts that may have become automatic. Carry a diary and write down these thoughts as soon as they cross your mind. This simple method will cast light on the thoughts, enabling you to generate distance.

(II) *Distancing and Correcting.* Once you've written down these thoughts, you've taken the first step toward challenging them. Instead of passively accepting these thoughts as truths, it's crucial that you question their accuracy. Ask yourself if there's evidence to support their validity. More often than not, you'll realize that you're being catastrophic due to a setback—and that's okay. We all slip into a fixed mindset from time to time. But we also have the responsibility to break free. These exercises, based on CBT, will guide you in this process.

Chapter Summary

- Some thoughts are more automatic than others. They run their course without you voluntarily wanting them to.
- Cognitive Behavioral Therapy (CBT) proposes that a way to change automatic thoughts, as fixed mindset thoughts can be, is to identify them, distance yourself from them, and challenge them.

- Mindset only matters in so far as it impacts your behavior.
- Grit is a better predictor of achievement than IQ, social intelligence, good looks, and physical health.
- The more intrinsically interested you are in an activity, and the more meaningful you find it, the grittier you will be.

8

DEVELOPING YOUR INTELLIGENCE IS A MORAL ACTION

I graduated high school hating the gray line that I thought judged me as forever insufficient, but graduated college third in a class of more than 150 students. In doing so, I saw both sides of the coin. High school teachers and students who looked at me over their shoulder and college professors who thought I had the natural gift of intelligence.

While I had received scholarships that smoothed the ride, I still had to pay for rent, food, and trips to Spain with money that I didn't have. I also naively thought that repaying my loan would not pose too much of an issue.

I failed to prepare for my landing in the job market, and during my last college year, I focused almost exclusively on classes rather than on job seeking. Together, these factors turned my stellar college career into a less stellar-sounding job: client service. But I didn't mind that, or so I thought.

If I had to guess, I'd say the average person gets called an asshole about five times per year. If that person is in the harsher sections of client service, the number probably skyrockets to at least five times per week.

"Here comes another foreigner on the phone. Do you even speak English?" was my bread and butter.

To deal with aggressive customers, some co-workers mentally reduced them to heavily troubled people— someone who, as they said, has issues and thus behaves irrationally. This approach is automatically dismissive, and if you want to maintain your sanity, it works.

If someone is shouting at you, mentally dismissing them as irrational is a protective strategy. Labeling someone as a crazy person means you don't have to listen to what they say and disentangle whatever issue may underlie the client's anger.

There was also the opposite extreme. Those who listened too much and accepted by default that whatever the aggressive client claimed was true. Inevitably, these co-workers were demolished whenever an insult came. "You are an asshole" is especially painful to hear if you assume the client speaks the truth just because they are The Client.

During my first few months at the job, I drifted from one extreme to the other. But one afternoon, my boss moved me next to a middle-aged co-worker, Deli, who had a reputation for being unintelligent, as she had severe trouble operating computers. And she did have computer-related issues, but as far as I could tell, Deli never lost her temper. Nor did she let herself go astray in tears, which was also common, especially among new employees.

Instead, Deli listened with empathy and almost always managed to disentangle why a client was being aggressive. Once she had figured that out, she would act right on that pain point to ease the client. Some were surprised when she got a much better-paying job months after joining our client service company. But I knew why.

As I learned from her, anger is not necessarily irrational, or rational, for that matter. Most angry clients were not crazy or speaking the full truth. Instead, they usually had a real problem and, like we all do, played their cards to solve it.

One customer had delayed rent payments and thus had a pressing landlord knocking on his door. In response, he tried to convince us that we had mistakenly overcharged his card for items he had not received (when it was clear he had). Another person was buying an expensive birthday gift to try to fix his relationship, and we were about to send that gift late because of New York's winter storms.

Unlike most of us, Deli searched for these problems when listening to clients. Her empathetic approach made her well-known around the office as a "good person." But nobody thought she was a good person and, therefore, smart.

"They're such a good person; they must be very smart" I bet you've never heard that.

"They aren't too bright, but at least they are good people..." You've probably heard some version of this sentence before.

As I first observed in client service, we tend to conceive morality as a motivational force. Whenever we judge someone as a good person, we seem to be saying that they are highly motivated to do good—that they have good intentions. But a wider conception of what it means to be a good person is more helpful.

Saying that someone is morally good and, therefore intelligent, sounds alien because we don't factor intelligence into morality. However, assuming the same motivation for moral action, the more intelligent you become, the more capacity you have for good. And empathy, which I argue is part of being a good person, is a good example.

As you know, displaying *empathy* requires putting yourself in someone else's shoes. But that's just a figure of speech. More specifically, to be empathetic involves *abstraction*. When you use empathy, you observe someone and build an accurate mental model of that person. Later, you construct a mental representation of the reality that person is in. Lastly, you play with that mental representation to understand, at an emotional level, how a situation impacts the person in front of you.

You are not that person and you are not in their situation. Yet, when you do it well, the emotional understanding derived from your mental model is very similar to what the actual person feels. And that leads to social connection. That's why Deli was so good with aggressive people. She could accurately build a mental representation of the person, the situation they were in, and understand what they were going through emotionally.

"I understand your issue, but we cannot help you at this moment." This is a version of what a client service representative who has not mastered empathy says.

"I understand your issue is *[detailed explanation of the issue and its emotional consequences]*, and *[proposed solution, even if it's just waiting for longer]*." This is an abstraction of what Deli would say.

Similarly, much of what makes for intelligence is the capacity for abstract reasoning. That same capacity makes for great mathematicians and philosophers. Of the kind that take the physical qualities of the world, abstract them, and mentally play with them through reasoning.

For instance, a number is an abstraction of an object in the physical world. A ball of clay in front of you gets abstractly represented as the mental symbol "1". A ball of clay coming together with another ball of clay to form a larger one (all physical objects) gets abstracted as "1+1 = 2 " (all abstract objects). These abstractions, as we've seen above, are not extremely different from what empathy requires that you do, making it a cognitively demanding operation.

Most scholars agree that empathy has this cognitive component.[1] In addition, neuroscientific studies have documented how empathy involves brain regions associated with abstract reasoning.[2] Together, parallels with math and evidence from neuroscience point to the idea that to be highly empathetic, you need to be at least somewhat smart.

On the contrary, being selfish doesn't require that you mentally represent another person, picture their situation, or emotionally understand what they are going through. Selfishness only requires that you act on your self-serving desires, which is a far cheaper cognitive operation. Perhaps that's why to be highly empathetic you need to be smart but to be selfish you can be an idiot.

Relatedly, with the accommodation of a growth mindset comes the development of your intelligence. And that requires that I make explicit something I've so far kept from mentioning: *Use this for good*.

The above has been an invisible line written underneath every chapter. Intelligence, when paired with good intentions, makes you a better person. But intelligence in itself has no moral color, it is merely brain power. As you become more capable, your capacity for moral action will increase, but so will your capacity for immoral action—and the temptation associated with that capacity.

A more intelligent computer scientist can innovate improved cybersecurity defenses, but they are also more apt to break cybersecurity walls and steal money. A more intelligent financial analyst can offer better advice to clients, but can also set up a more undetectable financial scam. You don't get the benefits derived from intelligence without the increased capability and temptation to misbehave.

Nothing in this book can prevent you from using the science of intellectual and skill development for self-serving desires and wrongdoing. To this end, all I can do is restate that within us, there's a conscience that speaks the language of regret when violated—unless you are biologically incapable of regret. That is, a psychopath.

Growth Mindset As Behavioral Law

As you become more skilled in a particular area, your mindset will evolve beyond mere thoughts. Initially, when facing a challenge in a relevant area, you might think, "I have what it takes to succeed," or "Why bother if I don't have the natural talent?"

These thoughts are normal but become less relevant as you master a craft; mastery turns thoughts into ingrained behavior. That is, you will no longer dwell on self-assessment during tasks. Instead, your focus will be entirely on the task itself.

"I don't have what it takes" or "I do have what it takes." These are just thoughts, and it is worth asking: What do your thoughts about yourself have to do with whatever task is in front of you? In a way, absolutely nothing.

I would find it rather distracting if, while writing, I started thinking about my writing ability. Instead, I seek a clear focus to immerse myself in the task. The growth mindset as an explicit thought is helpful when I hit a setback severe enough to break my focus. It reminds me that within a setback there is always an opportunity. Still, you can reach enough mastery in some specialized areas where you embody the growth mindset without actively thinking about it.

Thus, the notion that you can develop becomes implicit in your actions rather than explicit in your thoughts. In return, you will be fully immersed in the challenge at hand, directing *all* mental energy toward the task. The growth mindset will then turn into a behavioral law. And that will make you more competent because, as explicit thought, the growth mindset occupies mental capacity. But as behavioral law, it frees up capacity.

Doubting yourself or thinking yourself capable requires using some brain power to generate these thoughts. And there is an opportunity cost to every thought you generate. Necessarily, if you are thinking about yourself, you are not using that cognitive energy to think about the task at hand.

Doubts about your ability may still rise during periods of reflection or periods in which you are not performing well at a given task. That's where the growth mindset will help in the form of explicit thoughts. It will bring you back to the task.

Nonetheless, realize that if you adopt a growth mindset, reality will eventually pick you up. By adopting the reality-concordant belief that you can develop, in due time, you will fall flat on the fact that you are developing. Whether it is math, art, or sports, regardless of the area, if you adopt the growth mindset, the reality that you can develop will elevate your performance.

It is then a matter of time before the growth mindset is less needed in the form of explicit thought. To say it more poetically, the growth mindset will be in your bones, generating action, rather than in your mind, occupying space. At that very moment, it will turn into a law that guides your actions toward the proper challenges like gravity guides objects toward each other. And through these actions, you will collect the seeds of growth that challenges hold rather than the atrophy that avoidance returns.

Assuming you expose yourself to difficulties in the right dosage ("nothing in excess," said the entrance to Apollo's Temple), there is only one possible outcome to this process: human flourishing.

Beyond Escaping Misfortune

My visa was coming to an end. Four more months, and I would be kicked out of the United States. I had to get a job in the country or return to Spain. Either way, I had to find a way to repay my loan.

Looking for a job is a job in itself, and the client service hours were long. Those were stressful months, and all my attempts to get a long-term job in the United States came back as formal emails.

"You cost a lot of money to hire, sorry."

I had to look for a job in Spain and had to do it quickly. But a college education in the United States made it easier. After two months, I was offered a job in logistics in Seville. It was an offer that would allow me to repay my loan, so I accepted without hesitation. And after a year, I was free from debt.

By all my previous standards, I had made it. Everybody close to me shook my hand. But despite the good news, a sense of emptiness invaded me some days after paying off my last debt dollar.

Debtless, I could see that I had neglected a more meaningful pursuit than merely trying to avoid misfortune. I wanted to help my family and have a better future than unemployment, but I had failed to realize that we all have two mouths, one material, and one spiritual. The latter requires that we don't just run away from misfortune but also pursue a meaningful goal.

That higher goal had been paying off my debt and getting a safe job, but that was done. I had become confident enough in my ability that the unemployment monster didn't scare me so much. I had also developed enough confidence and ability to find a way out if my family or I ever lacked anything.

Without financial obligations beyond self-sustenance, the answer seemed clear: I had to find a goal brighter than escaping misfortune. But after years of education and work, I was clueless, completely lost, as to what that would be. I knew, however, that that higher goal wasn't in another stop in the corporate world.

My younger self would have thought this decision was straight madness. He would have been scared, but the source of my fears had changed. I quit the safe logistics job I had tirelessly pursued because, by then, I was more scared of an unfulfilled future than of material shortcomings.

I needed to figure out how to best live my professional life. And to find out, I talked to everybody I thought knew anything.

"If you get two things right," said my stats professors, "you'll only need to worry about sleeping well. One is what to do for work, the other is who you choose as a partner."

"Imagine," said my philosophy professor, "it's your birthday. You are about to go out with your friends to celebrate, but you've received an unexpected work-related call, and you have to stay. If you can, choose a job where this call would not be too demoralizing."

These were useful pieces of advice, but that's all they were. As far as the actual answer, only my hands could find it. Done with the corporate world, I set up an art business that failed to monetize. Wrote a book from my first memory to my last. Traveled to Madrid. Did psychology research at several labs. Traveled back to Seville. Taught Philosophy and English.

A deep enough dive into the ocean of experimentation made the answer as self-evident as an island to a castaway. In retrospect, it was obvious, but in forward motion barely anything is evident.

All of my rooms in Madrid, New York, and Seville were filled with piles of philosophy and psychology books. My school, client service, and logistics laptops had a small folder dedicated to classes and work. Surrounding that one folder were many more folders filled with essays, books, papers, and my own writing.

Experimentation had maximized the chances of finding a more meaningful path. It took me years, but I figured out that my career would be best lived if dedicated to what I do best: Research. Done with the thicker part of the fog, the next question was clear: Where can I do research?

Universities struck me as that place, so I allowed myself to think that a PhD program in the United States would want me. My younger and more fixed-mindset self, terrified of judgment and potential rejection, could never have dreamed of attempting anything like that, and no wonder.

It is scary to attempt hard work if it has a high chance of going unrewarded. But remember to reverse the picture. It is also scary to stay where you are if that's not where you want to be.

I got rejection letters, a few interviews, and more rejection letters. But, after enough rejection, Cornell University wanted the formerly failing high school student to join their psychology PhD program. I received the same congratulations as when I paid off my debt. This time, however, making its way through every good word, a sense of meaning rather than emptiness invaded me. As well as I could know something, I knew I had gotten the career part right.

To some of my high school peers, whom I see whenever I visit Madrid, I am the failing student. Barely making it on time to classes, tempted to falsify my parents' signature—more of a burden than a resource.

To some of my college peers, I am the "A" student. Always ready to face a challenge, always willing to go the extra mile—more capable of helping others. My story may vastly differ from yours, but we all have these two versions of ourselves. Only one of these versions, however, is capable of helping others.

If you develop your intelligence, you will be a more capable set of hands to any seeker of guidance and a better glue to any crumbling person, even when that person is yourself. Developing your intelligence increases your capacity to help others; that's why it's a moral action.

Action Steps

Problem-solving exercise:

(I) If you have a serious problem with someone, for instance, your partner, take a few minutes to write, as sincerely as you can, what you think your partner's point is. Don't write what you think their point *should* be or how they should see a situation. Instead, use your analytical capacity to write what you think their point *is*.

(II) Then, talk to the person with whom you have the problem and confirm that this is how they see the situation. If they agree, move forward to seek a solution. It is important that you only move forward in the discussion when the other person has confirmed that you are representing their point accurately.

(III) If you get stuck in the problem-solving process, go back to step (I). However, note that this is an infinite loop, and problems should not be kept infinitely. You can always part ways after attempting enough sensible solutions.

These steps are an adapted version of humanist psychologist Carl Rogers' approach to problem-solving.[3]

Chapter Summary

- Empathy requires abstraction, just like reasoning does.

- The areas of your brain associated with abstract reasoning are also active when you use empathy.
- The growth mindset as explicit thoughts is helpful, but as you master a craft, it will turn into a behavioral law or ingrained behavior.
- As behavioral law, the growth mindset frees up mental capacity, making you more efficient.
- Assuming enough motivation for moral action, the more intelligent you become, the better a person you will be.

AFTERWORD

Human flourishing, Aristotle thought, is the highest possible good achievable by action. And your thoughts, which can be controlled, significantly determine your actions.

Still, some things are outside of your control: your country of birth, your parents, and how much money your family has. These are relevant factors to achieve anything—we know that. But neglecting what's within your control because some things are outside of your control is not a sensible option.

Relatedly, the degree to which you flourish as a human being depends upon several factors. More narrowly, we have focused on developing intelligence and skills, which are also heavily impacted by your beliefs.

Since your beliefs fall within the controllable realm, you have some control over your intellectual and skill development. Thus, insofar as intellectual and skill development inform human flourishing, you have control over your own flourishing: You can take steps toward the highest of all goods, which is an incredibly optimistic fact about the human condition that is often underplayed.

To take steps toward flourishing, you must believe you can develop. But that, as we have covered, is an incomplete explanation. The growth mindset will maximize your development *not* because it is a positive attitude, a positive outlook on life, or a good-sounding slogan. The growth mindset will maximize your development because it is concordant with an underlying reality—because it holds truth. And truth is a necessary component for human flourishing.

The reality that underpins the growth mindset is brain plasticity. There will be areas where you have traditionally thought yourself untalented and incapable of development. Maybe you don't think you have the natural talents to be good at art, sports, or mathematics. Ultimately, all the activities you give yourself to are performed by your brain—a brain that has the capacity to develop. You do yourself and others a disservice by denying this underlying reality when doubting your capacity for development.

Rooted in falsehood, a fixed mindset will lead away from challenges and toward atrophy, and nothing worth attaining happens there. Just like truth is necessary for flourishing, falsehood, which the fixed mindset contains, is a pathway toward unnecessary suffering.

Truth, however, can be an abstract word that is hard to turn into action. But if you avoid falling in love with talent feedback and instead praise others for their effort; if you don't let the ghost of a narrative guide you without first casting light onto it; if you see failure as *not yet* and success as *so far*; if you can hold onto your humanity even under the perfect storm; if you don't automatically accept your thoughts but test their veracity; if you understand that developing your intelligence is a moral action; and if you allow truth rather than falsehood to be your soil, then, you will flourish. And there is no higher good than that.

THE PEOPLE BEHIND THINKNETIC

Christoph Maurer, Founder and CEO

Christoph has always been a voracious reader with a writing talent. A bit less common, he has also been fascinated by business since he was a child. Consequently, after earning his degree in business management, he chose publishing as a full-time career. With his good friend of over 15 years, Michael, he founded Thinknetic. The company aims to build the most reader-centric original publishing house possible and become a household brand trusted by its dear readers. Practicing what he preaches, Christoph spends a considerable amount of time reading every day, deeply influenced by the examples set by Charlie Munger and Warren Buffet.

Michael Meisner, Founder and CEO

When Michael ventured into publishing books on Amazon, he discovered that his favorite topics – the intricacies of the human mind and behavior – were often tackled in a way that's too complex and unengaging. Thus, he dedicated himself to making his ideal a reality: books that effortlessly inform, entertain, and resonate with readers' everyday experiences, enabling them to enact enduring positive changes in their lives.

Together with like-minded people, this ideal became his passion and profession. Michael is in charge of steering the strategic direction and brand orientation of Thinknetic, as he continues to improve and extend his business.

Farley Bermeo Jr., Publishing Manager

Farley has a knack for storytelling and writing personal narratives, both mundane and extraordinary. Combining his background in writing and experience in program management, he ensures that ideas are transformed into pages. He believes that a good story is better told with a cup of coffee.

Claire M. Umali, Publishing Manager

Collaborative work lies at the heart of crafting books, and keeping everyone on the same page is an essential task. Claire oversees all the stages of this collaboration, from researching to outlining and from writing to editing. In her free time, she writes online reviews and likes to bother her cats.

Daniel Martín-Alonso, Writer

Daniel is an author and PhD student in the Psychological Sciences and Human Development program at Cornell

University, where he studies decision-making. He has written extensively about human development, integrative approaches to autoimmune conditions, and philosophical examinations of life's meaning.

Grace Zaikoski, Content Editor

Grace Zaikoski is a Science Communications writer/editor. She graduated from Portland State University in 2014 with a B.A. in Science and works with hospitals, organizations, and professionals to share fact-based content with the everyday reader. She specializes in communicating medicine, science, and technology.

Sandra Agarrat, Language Editor

Sandra Wall Agarrat is an experienced freelance academic editor/proofreader, writer, and researcher. Sandra holds graduate degrees in Public Policy and International Relations. Her portfolio of projects includes books, dissertations, theses, scholarly articles, and grant proposals.

Danielle Contessa Tantuico, Researcher

Danielle conducts comprehensive research and develops outlines that are the backbone of Thinknetic's books. She finds pleasure in this role as it allows her to immerse herself in self-improvement topics. An avid reader and songwriter, Danielle channels her passion for artistic endeavors and personal growth into everything she creates for Thinknetic.

Yusra Rafiq, Copywriter

Yusra Rafiq, a freelance content alchemist, crafts content across diverse niches. Her expertise, honed over three years, encompasses writing, SEO optimization, and a spectrum of digital content. Beyond work, Yusra finds joy in family, pets, and love for documentaries, true crime, and sci-fi.

Jemarie Gumban, Hiring Manager

Jemarie is in charge of thoroughly examining and evaluating the profiles and potential of the many aspiring writers and associates for Thinknetic. With an academic background in Applied Linguistics and a meaningful experience as an industrial worker, she approaches her work with a discerning eye and fresh outlook. Guided by her unique perspective, Jemarie derives fulfillment from turning a writer's desire to create motivational literature into tangible reality.

Evangeline Obiedo, Publishing Assistant

Evangeline diligently supports our books' journey, from the writing stage to connecting with our readers. Her commitment to detail permeates her work, encompassing tasks such as initiating profile evaluations and ensuring seamless delivery of our newsletters. Her love for learning extends into the real world – she loves traveling and experiencing new places and cultures.

REFERENCES

The Highest Good

1. Aristotle (1925) The Nicomachean Ethics. *Oxford University Press, Oxford.* 4.

1. The Rarely Mentioned Reason Why Belief Matters

1. Mandler, G. (2011). *A history of modern experimental psychology: From James and Wundt to cognitive science.* MIT press.
2. Brentano, F., 1874 [1911, 1973, 1995], *Psychology from an Empirical Standpoint*, London: Routledge and Kegan Paul.
3. Dweck, C. (2008). Mindsets and Math/Science Achievement. New York: Carnegie Corporation of New York, Institute for Advanced Study, Commission on Mathematics and Science Education.
4. Voss, P., Thomas, M. E., Cisneros-Franco, J. M., & de Villers-Sidani, É. (2017). Dynamic brains and the changing rules of neuroplasticity: implications for learning and recovery. *Frontiers in psychology*, *8*, 1657.https://doi.org/10.3389/fpsyg.2017.01657

2. How To Breed A Quitter

1. Huberman Lab. (2022). Episode 56 – Dr. Alia Crum: Science of Mindsets for Health & Performance [Audio podcast]. Podcast Notes. Retrieved from https://podcastnotes.org/huberman-lab/episode-56-dr-alia-crum-science-of-mindsets-for-health-performance-huberman-lab/
2. Haidt, J., Rozin, P., McCauley, C., & Imada, S. (1997). Body, psyche, and culture: The relationship between disgust and morality. *Psychology and Developing Societies*, *9*(1), 107-131. https://doi.org/10.1177/097133369700900105
3. Ahn, W., & Perricone, A.M. (2023). Impacts of learning one's own genetic susceptibility to mental disorders. *Current Directions in Psychological Science.* 32(1), 42-48. Doi: 10.1177/09637214221127225

4. Serrano, J., with Martín-Alonso, D., Cruz, H. (2023). *Healing Is Possible. How to Heal Your Autoimmune Condition: The Integrative Approach That Is Helping Me Overcome Multiple Sclerosis.* Salud Autoimmune.

5. Cetin, B., Ilhan, M., & Yilmaz, F. (2014). An Investigation of the Relationship between the Fear of Receiving Negative Criticism and of Taking Academic Risk through Canonical Correlation Analysis. *Educational Sciences: Theory and Practice, 14*(1), 146-158. https://doi.org/10.12738/estp.2014.1.1616

6. Forsythe, A., & Johnson, S.W. (2017). Thanks, but no-thanks for the feedback. *Assessment & Evaluation in Higher Education*, 42, 850 - 859.

7. Mueller, C. M., & Dweck, C. S. (1998). Praise for intelligence can undermine children's motivation and performance. *Journal of Personality and Social Psychology, 75*(1), 33–52. https://doi.org/10.1037/0022-3514.75.1.33

8. Ryan, R. M., & Deci, E. L. (2000). Self-determination theory and the facilitation of intrinsic motivation, social development, and well-being. *American psychologist, 55*(1), 68. https://doi.org/10.1037/0003-066X.55.1.68

3. Everything You Impose Onto The World

1. World Bank(2020). International Labour Organization, Labour Force Statistics database (LFS). WorldBank. https://data.worldbank.org/indicator/SL.UEM.1524.NE.ZS?locations=ES

2. Boden, M. T., John, O. P., Goldin, P. R., Werner, K., Heimberg, R. G., & Gross, J. J. (2012). The role of maladaptive beliefs in cognitive-behavioral therapy: Evidence from social anxiety disorder. *Behaviour research and therapy, 50*(5), 287–291. https://doi.org/10.1016/j.brat.2012.02.007

3. Eurostat. (2023). *When do young Europeans leave their parental home?.* When do young Europeans leave their parental home? - Eurostat. https://ec.europa.cu/eur

4. Hirsh, J. B., Mar, R. A., & Peterson, J. B. (2013). Personal narratives as the highest level of cognitive integration. *The Behavioral and brain sciences, 36*(3), 216–217. https://doi.org/10.1017/S0140525X12002269

5. Gu, Y., Gu, S., Lei, Y., & Li, H. (2020). From Uncertainty to Anxiety: How Uncertainty Fuels Anxiety in a Process Mediated by Intolerance of Uncertainty. *Neural plasticity, 2020*, 8866386. https://doi.org/10.1155/2020/8866386

6. Masicampo, E. J., & Baumeister, R. F. (2011). Consider it done!

Plan-making can eliminate the cognitive effects of unfulfilled goals. *Journal of personality and social psychology*, *101*(4), 667.

7. Pennebaker, J. W., Kiecolt-Glaser, J. K., & Glaser, R. (1988). Disclosure of traumas and immune function: health implications for psychotherapy. *Journal of consulting and clinical psychology*, *56*(2), 239. (but also see, Mogk, C., Otte, S., Reinhold-Hurley, B., & Kröner-Herwig, B. (2006). Health effects of expressive writing on stressful or traumatic experiences-a meta-analysis. *GMS Psycho-Social Medicine*, *3*.)

8. Lung, C.T., & Dominowski, R.L. (1985). Effects of strategy instructions and practice on nine-dot problem solving. *Journal of Experimental Psychology: Learning, Memory, and Cognition*, *11*(4), 804-811.

9. Eliade, M. (1963). *Myth and reality*. (pp. 17-19). Harper & Row.

10. Lindow, J. (2002). *Norse mythology: A guide to gods, heroes, rituals, and beliefs*. Oxford University Press. 322-325

11. Levy, B. R., Slade, M. D., Murphy, T. E., & Gill, T. M. (2012). Association between positive age stereotypes and recovery from disability in older persons. *JAMA*, *308*(19), 1972–1973. https://doi.org/10.1001/jama.2012.14541

12. Levy, B. R., & Banaji, M. R. (2002). Implicit ageism. In T. D. Nelson (Ed.), *Ageism: Stereotyping and prejudice against older persons* (pp. 49–75). The MIT Press.

13. Levy, B. R., Slade, M. D., Kunkel, S. R., & Kasl, S. V. (2002). Longevity increased by positive self-perceptions of aging. *Journal of personality and social psychology*, *83*(2),261–270.https://doi.org/10.1037//0022-3514.83.2.261

14. Crum, A. J., Salovey, P., & Achor, S. (2013). Rethinking stress: the role of mindsets in determining the stress response. *Journal of personality and social psychology, 104(4), 716.*

15. Bidlingmaier, M., & Strasburger, C. J. (2010). Growth hormone. *Doping in Sports: Biochemical Principles, Effects and Analysis*, 187-200.

16. Benedetti, F., Maggi, G., Lopiano, L., Lanotte, M., Rainero, I., Vighetti, S., & Pollo, A. (2003). Open versus hidden medical treatments: The patient's knowledge about a therapy affects the therapy outcome. *Prevention & Treatment*, *6*(1), 1a.

17. Planès, S., Villier, C., & Mallaret, M. (2016). The nocebo effect of drugs. *Pharmacology research & perspectives*, *4*(2),e00208. https://doi.org/10.1002/prp2.208

18. Mitsikostas, D. D., Mantonakis, L. I., & Chalarakis, N. G. (2011). Nocebo is the enemy, not placebo. A meta-analysis of reported side effects after placebo treatment in headaches. Cephalalgia, 31(5), 550-561.

19. Papadopoulos, D., & Mitsikostas, D. D. (2012). A meta-analytic approach to estimating nocebo effects in neuropathic pain trials. Journal of neurology, 259(3), 436–447. https://doi.org/10.1007/s00415-011-6197-4
20. Häuser, W., Sarzi-Puttini, P., Tölle, T. R., & Wolfe, F. (2012). Placebo and nocebo responses in randomised controlled trials of drugs applying for approval for fibromyalgia syndrome treatment: systematic review and meta-analysis. Clinical and experimental rheumatology, 30(6 Suppl 74), 78–87.

4. Choose Your Responses Wisely

1. Mandler, G. (2011). *A history of modern experimental psychology: From James and Wundt to cognitive science.* MIT press.
2. Staddon, J. E., & Cerutti, D. T. (2003). Operant conditioning. *Annual review of psychology, 54*(1), 115-144.
3. Skinner, B. F. (2005). Walden two. Hackett Publishing.
4. Ibid., 10
5. Skinner, B. F. (1948). 'Superstition' in the pigeon. Journal of Experimental Psychology, 38(2), 168–172. https://doi.org/10.1037/h0055873
6. Puhl, M. D., Blum, J. S., Acosta-Torres, S., & Grigson, P. S. (2012). Environmental enrichment protects against the acquisition of cocaine self-administration in adult male rats, but does not eliminate avoidance of a drug-associated saccharin cue. Behavioural pharmacology, 23(1), 43–53. https://doi.org/10.1097/FBP.0b013e32834eb060
7. Venniro, M., Zhang, M., Caprioli, D., Hoots, J. K., Golden, S. A., Heins, C., Morales, M., Epstein, D. H., & Shaham, Y. (2018). Volitional social interaction prevents drug addiction in rat models. *Nature neuroscience, 21*(11), 1520–1529. https://doi.org/10.1038/s41593-018-0246-6
8. Puhl, M. D., Blum, J. S., Acosta-Torres, S., & Grigson, P. S. (2012). Environmental enrichment protects against the acquisition of cocaine self-administration in adult male rats, but does not eliminate avoidance of a drug-associated saccharin cue. Behavioural pharmacology, 23(1), 43–53. https://doi.org/10.1097/FBP.0b013e32834eb060
9. Compas, B. E., Jaser, S. S., Bettis, A. H., Watson, K. H., Gruhn, M. A., Dunbar, J. P., Williams, E., & Thigpen, J. C. (2017). Coping, emotion regulation, and psychopathology in childhood and

adolescence: A meta-analysis and narrative review. *Psychological bulletin, 143*(9), 939–991. https://doi.org/10.1037/bul0000110

10. Compas, B. E., Jaser, S. S., Bettis, A. H., Watson, K. H., Gruhn, M. A., Dunbar, J. P., Williams, E., & Thigpen, J. C. (2017). Coping, emotion regulation, and psychopathology in childhood and adolescence: A meta-analysis and narrative review. *Psychological bulletin, 143*(9), 939–991. https://doi.org/10.1037/bul0000110

11. Frankl, V. E. 1. (1984). *Man's search for meaning: an introduction to logotherapy.* (p. 48). New York, Simon & Schuster.

12. Ibid., 70

13. Carver, C. S. (1997). You want to measure coping but your protocol is too long: Consider the brief cope. *International journal of behavioral medicine, 4*(1), 92-100.

5. Walking A Fine Line

1. *A Choice of Kipling's Verse* (1943).

2. Garland E. L. (2012). Pain processing in the human nervous system: a selective review of nociceptive and biobehavioral pathways. *Primary care, 39*(3), 561–571. https://doi.org/10.1016/j.pop.2012.06.013

3. Bentham, J. (1996). *The collected works of Jeremy Bentham: An introduction to the principles of morals and legislation.* Clarendon Press.

6. On Brain Plasticity. Why You Are (Probably) Not A Zebra

1. Turrigiano, G. G. (2008). The self-tuning neuron: synaptic scaling of excitatory synapses. *Cell, 135*(3), 422-435.

2. Ben-Dor, M., Sirtoli, R., & Barkai, R. (2021). The evolution of the human trophic level during the pleistocene. *American Journal of Physical Anthropology, 175*(S72), 27–56. https://doi.org/10.1002/ajpa.24247

3. Cassinello, J. (2021). The human Hunter as predator: A new role under a food web restoration scenario. *Journal of Arid Environments, 186*, 104420. https://doi.org/10.1016/j.jaridenv.2020.104420

4. Gómez-Robles, A., & Sherwood, C. C. (2016). Human brain evolution: How the increase of brain plasticity made us a cultural species. *Mètode Revista de Difusió de La Investigació, 0*(7). https://doi.org/10.7203/metode.7.7602

5. Voss, P., Thomas, M. E., Cisneros-Franco, J. M., & de Villers-Sidani, É. (2017). Dynamic brains and the changing rules of

neuroplasticity: implications for learning and recovery. *Frontiers in psychology, 8*, 1657.https://doi.org/10.3389/fpsyg.2017.01657

6. Gómez-Robles, A., Nicolaou, C., Smaers, J. B., & Sherwood, C. C. (2024). The evolution of human altriciality and brain development in comparative context. *Nature ecology & evolution, 8*(1), 133–146. https://doi.org/10.1038/s41559-023-02253-z

7. Serrano, J., Martin-Alonso, D., & Cruz, H., (2023). *Healing Is Possible. How to Heal Your Autoimmune Condition: The Integrative Method That Is Helping Me Overcome Multiple Sclerosis.* Salud Autoimmune

8. Spalding, K. L., Bergmann, O., Alkass, K., Bernard, S., Salehpour, M., Huttner, H. B., Boström, E., Westerlund, I., Vial, C., Buchholz, B. A., Possnert, G., Mash, D. C., Druid, H., & Frisén, J. (2013). Dynamics of hippocampal neurogenesis in adult humans. Cell, 153(6), 1219–1227. https://doi.org/10.1016/j.cell.2013.05.002

9. Public Domain Media Search Engine. (1941, January 1). *Thousands of books smoulder in a huge bonfire as Germans give the Nazi salute during the wave of book-burnings that... - nara - 535791 - picryl - public domain media search engine public domain search.* PICRYL.https://picryl.com/media/thousands-of-books-smoulder-in-a-huge-bonfire-as-germans-give-the-nazi-salute-b1f036

10. Public Domain Media Search Engine. (1933, May 6). *Nazi reading before burning the library of dr. Hirschfeld, Institute for Sexual Research, Berlin, 6 May 1933- institut für Sexualwissenschaft - Bibliothek 1933 (cropped) - picryl - public domain media search engine public domain search.*PICRYL.https://picryl.com/media/nazi-reading-before-burning-the-library-of-dr-hirschfeld-institute-for-sexual-2318dc

11. United States Holocaust Memorial Museum. (n.d.). United States holocaust memorial museum. https://encyclopedia.ushmm.org/content/en/article/nazi-propaganda-and-censorship

12. Cotman, C. W., & Berchtold, N. C. (2002). Exercise: a behavioral intervention to enhance brain health and plasticity. *Trends in neurosciences, 25*(6), 295-301.

13. Cross, A., & Sheffield, D. (2019). Mental contrasting for health behaviour change: a systematic review and meta-analysis of effects and moderator variables. *Health Psychology Review, 13*(2), 209-225.

14. Manini, T. M., Yarrow, J. F., Buford, T. W., Clark, B. C., Conover, C. F., & Borst, S. E. (2012). Growth hormone responses to acute resistance exercise with vascular restriction in young and old men. *Growth hormone & IGF research : official journal of the Growth Hormone Research Society and the International IGF Research Society, 22*(5), 167–172. https://doi.org/10.1016/j.ghir.2012.05.002

7. Overcoming Sticky Thoughts And Accomplishing Big Goals

1. Freud, S. (1983). 2. The Interpretation of Dreams. In E. Kurzweil & W. Phillips (Ed.), *Literature and Psychoanalysis (pp. 29-33).* New York Chichester, West Sussex: Columbia University Press. https://doi.org/10.7312/kurz91842-004
2. Beck, A. T. (1970). Cognitive therapy: Nature and relation to behavior therapy. *Behavior therapy,* 1(2), 184-200.
3. Duckworth, A. L., Peterson, C., Matthews, M. D., & Kelly, D. R. (2007). Grit: perseverance and passion for long-term goals. *Journal of personality and social psychology,* 92(6), 1087.
4. Epigenetic Tips. (2023). *Andrew Huberman: "this is the holy grail of neuroscience!"* YouTube. https://www.youtube.com/watch?app=desktop&v=MvoOVYrNZRs
5. Martín, S. (1980). *Relatos de Mazagatos.*
6. Lao, J. R., & Young, J. (2019). *Resistance to belief change: Limits of learning.* Routledge.
7. Duckworth, A. L., Quirk, A., Gallop, R., Hoyle, R. H., Kelly, D. R., & Matthews, M. D. (2019). Cognitive and noncognitive predictors of success. *Proceedings of the National Academy of Sciences,* 116(47), 23499-23504.
8. Duckworth, A. (2016). Grit: The power of passion and perseverance (Vol. 234). *New York, NY: Scribner.*
9. Commisso, M., & Finkelstein, L. (2012). Physical attractiveness bias in employee termination. *Journal of Applied Social Psychology,* 42(12), 2968-2987.
10. Martín-Alonso, D. *(forthcoming).* *To K*ll Oneself Or To Eat Stew In Madrid. An Essay On The Meaning Of Life.*
11. Martín-Alonso, D. (2021). How To Know If You Are Biased. Mathematical Models to Disentangle Control in Implicit Measures. *Behavioral Sciences Conference.*

8. Developing Your Intelligence Is A Moral Action

1. Decety J. (2010). The neurodevelopment of empathy in humans. *Developmental neuroscience,* 32(4), 257–267. https://doi.org/10.1159/000317771
2. Light, S. N., Coan, J. A., Zahn-Waxler, C., Frye, C., Goldsmith, H. H., & Davidson, R. J. (2009). Empathy is associated with dynamic

change in prefrontal brain electrical activity during positive emotion in children. *Child development, 80*(4), 1210–1231. https://doi.org/10.1111/j.1467-8624.2009.01326.x

3. Rogers, C. R. (1995). *On becoming a person: A therapist's view of psychotherapy*. Houghton Mifflin Harcourt.

DISCLAIMER

The information contained in this book and its components, is meant to serve as a comprehensive collection of strategies that the author of this book has done research about. Summaries, strategies, tips and tricks are only recommendations by the author, and reading this book will not guarantee that one's results will exactly mirror the author's results.

The author of this book has made all reasonable efforts to provide current and accurate information for the readers of this book. Names and basic facts have been changed in these stories and any similarity to actual persons, living or dead, is purely coincidental. The author and their associates will not be held liable for any unintentional errors or omissions that may be found, and for damages arising from the use or misuse of the information presented in this book.

Readers should exercise their own judgment and discretion in interpreting and applying the information to their specific circumstances. This book is not intended to replace professional advice (especially medical advice, diagnosis, or treatment). Readers are encouraged to seek appropriate professional guidance for their individual needs.

The material in the book may include information by third parties. Third party materials comprise of opinions expressed by their owners. As such, the author of this book does not assume responsibility or liability for any third party material or opinions.

The publication of third party material does not constitute the author's guarantee of any information, products, services, or opinions contained within third party material. Use of third party material does not guarantee that your results will mirror our results. Publication of such third party material is simply a recommendation and expression of the author's own opinion of that material.

Whether because of the progression of the Internet, or the unforeseen changes in company policy and editorial submission guidelines, what is stated as fact at the time of this writing may become outdated or inapplicable later.

Thinknetic is committed to respecting copyright laws and intellectual property rights. We have taken reasonable measures to ensure that all quotes, diagrams, figures, images, tables, and other information used in this publication are either created by us, obtained with permission, or fall under fair use guidelines. However, if any copyright infringement has inadvertently occurred, please notify us promptly, providing sufficient details to identify the specific material in question. We will take immediate action to rectify the situation, which may include obtaining necessary permissions, making corrections, or removing the material in subsequent editions or reprints.

This book is copyright ©2023 by Thinknetic with all rights reserved. It is illegal to redistribute, copy, or create derivative works from this book whole or in parts. No parts of this report may be reproduced or retransmitted in any forms whatsoever without the written expressed and signed permission from the publisher.

Printed in Great Britain
by Amazon

57505302R00108